THE POWER OF HOPE

THE POWER OF HOPE

Thoughts on Peace and Human Rights in the Third Millennium

DAISAKU IKEDA
and
ADOLFO PÉREZ ESQUIVEL

I.B. TAURIS

LONDON • NEW YORK • OXFORD • NEW DELHI • SYDNEY

I.B. TAURIS

Bloomsbury Publishing Plc

50 Bedford Square, London, WC1B 3DP, UK

1385 Broadway, New York, NY 10018, USA

29 Earlsfort Terrace, Dublin 2, Ireland

BLOOMSBURY, I.B. TAURIS and the I.B. Tauris logo are trademarks of Bloomsbury Publishing Plc

First published in Great Britain 2021

Cover design by ianrossdesigner.com
Cover image (c) Seikyo Shimbun

Bloomsbury Publishing Plc does not have any control over, or responsibility for, any third-party websites referred to or in this book. All internet addresses given in this book were correct at the time of going to press. The author and publisher regret any inconvenience caused if addresses have changed or sites have ceased to exist, but can accept no responsibility for any such changes.

A catalogue record for this book is available from the British Library.

A catalog record for this book is available from the Library of Congress.

ISBN: HB: 978-0-7556-0639-9
       PB: 978-0-7556-0640-5
       ePDF: 978-0-7556-0641-2
       eBook: 978-0-7556-0642-9

Typeset by RefineCatch Limited, Bungay, Suffolk

To find out more about our authors and books visit www.bloomsbury.com and sign up for our newsletters.

Contents

Foreword

The heart is free and unfettered; it can reach out and commune with another, regardless of what geographic distance may separate the two. Viewed from Argentina, Japan literally lies on the opposite side of the Earth. Yet, though I may live in Japan, no country is closer to my heart than Argentina. This is because her sheer natural beauty, her dynamic culture, shine in my heart in all their glorious splendor. But most important of all, I feel this way because a kindred spirit of mine resides there.

My first encounter with Dr. Adolfo Pérez Esquivel and his beloved wife, Amanda, two dear friends for whom my admiration knows no bounds, took place in Tokyo on December 8, 1995. Genuine friendship never wanes with the passage of time; indeed, its candescence only grows stronger. That has been the case with my friendship with Dr. Esquivel.

When the Tohoku earthquake and tsunami struck in March 2011, Dr. Esquivel was among the very first to send a message to me, sharing his deeply felt solidarity:

> If there is anything we can do, please do not hesitate to let us know. I offer my heartfelt prayers that all of you will face your plight with hope and stout hearts.

Dr. Esquivel pays no heed to borders that divide nations. Neither geographical distance, cultural barriers, nor ethnic differences can prevent him from reaching out to the suffering. He always sides with young people who are battling adversity. Whatever hardship they are facing—disasters, wars, violence, famine, inequality, oppression, poverty—he is there fighting alongside the ordinary citizens, taking that first step in breaking through any impasse toward hope.

With his conscience as his compass, he refuses to turn away from people in distress. Holding an abiding faith in the capacity of ordinary people to prevail over difficulty, he stands at the forefront of their struggle, showing them the way to draw forth that capacity. This is a path that only the most intrepid and pertinacious dare walk.

In the battle against iniquity, to speak out for the sake of a public in distress means to invite perilous reprisal. It was precisely because of Dr. Esquivel's steadfast commitment to the cause of peace and justice that a tyrannical regime baselessly accused him of crimes and imprisoned him. And yet, though it nearly cost him his life, he would not bow to his oppressors, prevailing in the end and ultimately being awarded the Nobel Peace Prize, earning the acclaim of millions.

His words are therefore ones uttered by an individual who has walked the harsh, unforgiving path of experience. They are eloquent truths that can only be spoken by a champion who has risked his own life. That is why I have shared them with others on every possible occasion.

He is of the conviction that everyone should have someone to look to as a spiritual bulwark and role model in life. However, rather than citing some prominent historical personage, Dr. Esquivel points to his grandmother as the person whom he finds the most heroic, a woman of goodness whose name history will never chronicle. Many of my friends in Japan and around the world have been profoundly moved to hear this.

So, may I proudly declare: There is no greater champion of the people than Dr. Esquivel himself.

Dr. Esquivel and his wife are artists who relish engaging in creative endeavors. I consider my frank and broad discourses with him on the cultures of Latin America, Asia, and the world to be among the most enjoyable I have ever experienced.

Culture is the struggle of humanity against barbarity. This is why I hold that the communion of cultures is foundational to genuine peace. I am determined to strive ever harder to deepen understanding among all cultures and to facilitate exchange among them, taking the friendship between Argentina and Japan, which dates back more than a century, as a point from which to begin. I do so in an effort to establish even stronger bonds that can bring the hearts and minds of people everywhere closer together.

Dr. Esquivel and I have both reached an age where we must convey our efforts to advance peace, our struggles for human rights and to build solidarity among cultures—causes to which we have committed our entire lives—so that younger generations may carry our legacies forward.

It is not in order that I myself may flower that I till the soil of self-actualization. Instead, I am resolved to lay down my life as the earth and foundation from which the young people who are to succeed me may flourish.

Dr. Esquivel's heart has been equally firm, striking out to this day to forge a path where none existed before. He has stated that he did so with the resolve to leave behind a testimony of his struggle and resistance against oppression and to set an example for those to follow.

Every youth, wherever you may be, that is where you must make a stand and fulfill your purpose in life—for your own self-development, for the sake of others, and for justice and peace. This may at times demand something as valiant as to stake your very life; or it may demand the kind of unrelenting effort that uses up every ounce of your energy.

Still, I believe young people, when introduced to Dr. Esquivel's life of struggle and triumph, will draw boundless encouragement from the existence of a man who continues to lead so many others by fearlessly dedicating his entire being to his struggle. I am confident that the reader will be able to find unlimited courage and hope in the words of conviction that he shares in this work.

In the Lotus Sutra, which many hold to be the heart of the Mahayana teachings of Buddhism, the bodhisattvas entrusted to guide people to enlightenment are described as emerging from the earth in procession, dancing with joy.

It is my undying hope that the youth who follow in the footsteps of the always spirited Dr. Esquivel will rise joyously from the Mother Earth of South America, the Mother Earth of the world. May they all stand someday like the Andes, a mighty procession of capable individuals who tower majestically as a bulwark of peace.

In closing, I offer my heartfelt prayers for the continued good health of Dr. Esquivel and Mrs. Amanda Esquivel, and that the esteemed Argentine Republic will shine evermore in peerless glory.

Daisaku Ikeda

Foreword
Dialogue with Maestro Daisaku Ikeda

Rivers tread a vast distance from the mountains down to the plains, traversing deserts and jungles toward a common destination, snaking their way across the land until they are embraced by the great sea. Along the journey, they leave trails across time, pour memories into troubled waters, reveal their faces over cascading waterfalls, or illuminate their depths in clear, calm ponds. Over the ceaseless course of time, Mother Earth nurtures life, transcending all changes, offering her bountiful gifts to her countless sons and daughters and to every living being. Humanity has long walked between rivers of light and shadow, cultivating the power of words and life force, sowing the land of history with grief and killing but also with seeds of hope and life for all.

We need to listen to the words brought from afar by the four winds—the testimony of our ancestors who bequeathed their knowledge for the sake of their peoples, whose voices have woven the tapestry of collective memory—in the awareness that there is no memory without the past, and no past without the future. We need to restore harmony and balance within ourselves and with the world in which we live, acknowledging that a single drop of water contains the entire river and that all rivers exist in each single droplet. We are a small part of the whole and the whole itself at the same time. This entails learning to recognize ourselves in the singularity and diversity of life, which endlessly weaves the warp and woof of culture, society, and spirituality. And, also, to perpetuate values from one generation to the next.

From time to time, the deep riverbeds of life give birth to people who are architects of conscience, sculptors of words spoken from the heart, and tillers of thought that bear fruit and flower in the vast earth of humanity. Maestro Daisaku Ikeda is one of those founding builders whose life has opened roads to peace through his day-to-day struggle, in a ceaseless quest of spirituality and education, channeled and enhanced through the endeavors of the Soka Gakkai International.

I met Maestro Ikeda and his wife, Kaneko, accompanied by representatives of Soka University, during one of my visits to Tokyo. I could immediately sense his deep diligence and wisdom nurtured by Buddhism, as well as his educational and philosophical thought, his openness to engage in a collaborative understanding of diverse cultural and social voices. I also appreciated his keen and informed interest in Latin America and his focus on youth, as well as his social commitment to peacebuilding, with a concerned eye to the needs of those left behind. Through the years, we have come to know each other and, in the confluence of our respective paths in life, we have joined in a shared navigation along the broad current of peace, human dignity, and deep devotion to Mother Nature.

Maestro Ikeda is a man of unflinching confidence. This conviction is born from the hope and the knowledge that humanity can achieve positive and better changes, both for the individual and for society, despite the challenges posed by wars, conflicts, hunger, or poverty.

Before we had met in person, I had been an honored guest at various Soka Gakkai activities in Buenos Aires, where I was able to grasp a strong commitment to the fostering of social, cultural, and spiritual values. I witnessed the laudable work of local members in different communities across the country, following and putting into practice both the teachings of Nichiren Buddhism and Maestro Ikeda's guidance in their thoughts and words. These members are also building a network of dialogue, solidarity, and service together with their fellow citizens based on promoting awareness and taking positive action.

With philosophy and spirituality as his source, Maestro Ikeda opens up his heart through dialogue and action, toward horizons of mutual knowledge. In our personal encounters and, later, making use of technology for remote communication, we have developed a deep exchange about pressing issues that pose a threat to our world and our peoples. From this starting point, and as we shared our life experiences, we have naturally expanded our discussions to include civic and human rights, pathways to peace, and the challenges of the twenty-first century. We have done so with the spirit of creating a message that could be inherited by new generations and that may contribute to the promotion of reflection and commitment for the sake of all peoples.

The fruits of our dialogue, sustained over the years, resemble a message borne by the currents of a river as it flows. I hope our discourse will help to remind us that life is full of unexpected amazement, that our hearts will always retain the sensitivity to admire an adorable flower, a charming smile, a gorgeous sunset, even if we cannot explain why they are beautiful as a work of creation. We are moved by their beauty just because they stir our hearts and awaken our conscience. And this reminds us to be "awake," to truly look and listen. As the ancient proverb goes, "The fish cannot see the waters in which they live."

Japan and Argentina in far-off Latin America are geographically distant and have contrasting heritages in terms of thought, culture, and spirituality. Nevertheless, Maestro Ikeda and I feel as close as siblings, knowing that distance vanishes when words flow, when values and memories are shared and when we are united by a common spiritual heritage of wisdom accrued over the centuries. These are the sources of the seas and rivers that gather together and rejoin in the oneness of the universe.

Adolfo Pérez Esquivel

To the Youth of the World

An Appeal for Resilience and Hope—by
Adolfo Pérez Esquivel and Daisaku Ikeda
(Rome, June 5, 2018)

(On June 5, 2018, in Rome, Italy, Nobel Peace Prize Laureate Adolfo Pérez Esquivel and Buddhist philosopher Daisaku Ikeda released a joint appeal to young people worldwide, calling for a new world built on justice and solidarity.)

We call on the young people of the world to unite to meet the challenges confronting humankind, to be the authors of their own lives and of the history of the new century. Our hope is infinite because we believe that youth will know how to resolve the many diverse planetary challenges in solidarity. We direct this message to young people, in whom we place our total confidence.

In the twenty-first century, humankind confronts a vertiginous dynamic of change, which brings with it immense challenges.

It is necessary to remember history. Such memory illuminates the present. Through it, we can see that people have the capacity and the strength to create new alternatives and to be beacons of hope demonstrating that "another world is possible."

The twentieth century, its light and shadow, left profound marks on human history, generating asymmetries and injustice between so-called developed and developing societies, as well as growing wealth gaps within all societies.

Hunger is a crime. Combating poverty and hunger is essential. In order to eliminate misery from Earth, we must transcend differences of nationality, ethnicity, religion and culture, coming together in support of the United Nations 2030 Agenda for Sustainable Development and its goal of "transforming our world."

The Challenge of a New Era

Advances have been made toward the creation of a new era. One of these was the Paris Agreement, which established measures to combat climate change. Against the backdrop of the growing threat of extreme weather events and rising sea levels, the agreement entered into force in November 2016 and has been ratified by almost all of the world's countries.

Another step forward was the adoption of the Treaty on the Prohibition of Nuclear Weapons in July 2017, an international legal instrument that establishes the absolute illegality of these weapons.

In November 2017, the international symposium "Perspectives for a World Free from Nuclear Weapons and for Integral Disarmament" was convened by Pope Francis at the Vatican. In pursuing the goal of a world without nuclear weapons, we must eliminate not only the threat these weapons pose, but also the urge to power and the desire to realize security for one's own country even at the expense of the lives and the dignity of other peoples. There is an urgent need to disarm our ways of thinking.

The two of us have discussed global issues motivated by an unchanging and unbounded faith in the potential of youth.

We have seen how young people worldwide worked as key agents of civil society in solidarity with the International Campaign to Abolish Nuclear Weapons (ICAN) to propel the adoption of the Treaty on the Prohibition of Nuclear Weapons in 2017.

The future of humankind depends on the present, on young people who have the courage to confront reality, never submitting before adversity.

As Martin Luther King Jr. said, "We are always on the threshold of a new dawn." In this spirit, the two of us embrace the confidence that there exists always the hope and the will to bring about a new dawn for humankind and for the living beings with whom we share this planet Earth as our common home.

The refugee problem has reached crisis proportions. The lives and dignity of tens of millions of people are violated by war and armed conflict, starvation, social and structural violence. We must open our arms, minds and hearts in solidarity with the most vulnerable in order to rectify this grave situation.

Our Message to Youth

We direct our call to the young people of the world. There is no challenge that cannot be resolved if we unite in solidarity. We are confident that young people will take up the search for solutions, acting in solidarity from within their respective places of belonging across all differences of spiritual and cultural identity to generate waves of dynamic, shared action. We call on youth to take on the responsibility of walking together with the people, embracing the confidence that each of their actions will produce results in future.

The threat of nuclear weapons, the increasing number of refugees driven from their homes by armed conflict, extreme weather events caused by climate change, the greed of financial speculators that aggravates the gap between rich and poor . . . Underneath these problems lies an unrestrained vying for military, political and economic supremacy that casts dark shadows over our common home, our planet Earth.

There is a worrying trend in society: the extreme and unbridled ambition for power and wealth that embodies the belief that it should be possible to obtain all things quickly and easily.

Eastern philosophy teaches that such benightedness is generated by three negative impulses: greed driven by runaway egotism, anger that gives rise to hatred and conflict with others, and ignorance that causes us to lose our sense of direction in life and society.

Mahatma Gandhi urged people to evaluate their words and actions by reflecting on the impact they could have on others, bringing to mind the faces of the poorest and most vulnerable among us. Gandhi was convinced that each society should develop keeping in mind the welfare of the most disadvantaged, never abandoning anyone. This perspective accords with the humanistic ideal of the United Nations Sustainable Development Goals (SDGs), to "leave no one behind."

Appeal to International Society

With this joint appeal, we call for restraint of the excesses of civilization and a restoring of equilibrium between human beings and Mother Earth. We call on international society to promote the empowerment of young people through education for global citizenship in order to lay the foundation for truly inclusive societies.

We propose the implementation of a range of new efforts aimed at fostering global citizens toward the year 2030 and at empowering youth by unleashing their unlimited capacities and potential.

These efforts should:

1. Promote a common awareness of a universal sense of history in order to prevent the repetition of tragedies.
2. Promote the understanding that Earth is our common home, where no one is to be excluded on the basis of difference.
3. Promote the humane orientation of politics and economics, cultivating the wisdom needed to achieve a sustainable future.

In achieving these three objectives, it is vital that young people unite in solidarity, generating a powerful dynamic of action to meet planetary challenges and protect Mother Earth.

With the Torch Held High

The two of us have lived through the storms of war and violence of the twentieth century. These experiences drive our insistent efforts to expand the bonds of friendship among peoples across ethnic and religious differences. We now feel compelled to reach out to the youth of the twenty-first century and to entrust to them the task of holding high, with courage and pride, the torch of friendship, unity in diversity.

We consider it to be of the greatest importance to human society today and in the future that young people commit themselves to working with the world's peoples to usher in a new dawn of hope; that they unite in solidarity to protect the dignity of life, fight injustice and make equally accessible those things that are necessary for people's physical and spiritual existence in freedom. By doing this, young people will create a precious and universal spiritual heritage for humankind, a new world of justice and solidarity.

(This text, originally released on June 5, 2018, is reproduced from the Daisaku Ikeda website {www. daisakuikeda.org}.

This dialogue was originally serialized in the
Japanese edition of *The Journal of Oriental Studies,*
a biannual journal of the Institute of Oriental
Philosophy, in four installments from December 2006
to May 2008. It was published in book form in
Japanese edition as *Jinken no seiki eno messeiji*
(A Message to the Century of Human Rights) in 2009.
It was also re-edited and supplemented with
additional passages, and published as *La Fuerza de la
Esperanza* (The Power of Hope) in Spanish in 2011.

ONE

The Struggle for Human Rights— A Story of Glorious Triumph

Bringing an End to the Suffering of the People

Ikeda: I greatly respect people who stand up for the dignity of humanity and strive to reform our times through concrete actions.

You are such a person, and one of the precious treasures of our world.

Refusing to be defeated by the relentless oppression of a military dictatorship, you have remained true to your belief in justice. At the risk of your very life, you have exerted the most strenuous efforts for the sake of peace. Your life sends forth a ray of courage and hope for humanity.

That is why I am delighted to have this opportunity to engage in this dialogue with you.

Esquivel: As am I, President Ikeda. Thank you for this opportunity.

As a reader of your writings, I have looked forward to meeting you in person and feel I have already known you for a long time.

Ikeda: I feel the same. I wholeheartedly applauded your receipt of the Nobel Peace Prize in 1980, at the age of forty-nine.

On that occasion, the Nobel Committee explained their choice, praising you as "an untiring and consistent champion of the principle of nonviolence" who "has lit a light in the dark."[1]

Your nonviolent struggle will shine forever as a triumph of the human spirit in the twentieth and twenty-first centuries.

Esquivel: I thank you for your esteem and words of appreciation.

All human beings are born with equal rights. Thus they have the capability to choose their own way of life, to exercise their freedom, and to select their chosen path. Unfortunately, however, many are denied these fundamental rights. When we examine human history, that is, the actual lives of the ordinary people, we see faces convulsed in suffering.

Great numbers of people are born under a death sentence due to hunger and war; others are born into conditions on a par with slavery, the suffering of poverty, or social exclusion.

These people have no ways out of their situations.

They are in need of friendly hands extended by those around them and the people of the world to support them and move forward with them in solidarity. Millions of people on Earth are clamoring for a more just and humane way of life.

Ikeda: Human history has been too full of misery caused by war, violence, discrimination, and oppression. Yet still these tragedies continue, as if we haven't undergone enough.

Now in the twenty-first century humanity must look directly at the path it has followed so far and, with a view to the third millennium, blaze the correct path forward. I believe this is the obligatory mission and duty of those of us alive today.

We must build a society based on respect for human dignity. We must make the shift from an age of authoritarian control to one of the autonomy of the people. And we must transition to a society in which the full potential of women is allowed to shine on the stage of history.

All of these are daunting challenges, major transformations of human history. I wish to engage with you, Dr. Esquivel, in the challenge of finding the ways to effect that transformation.

Esquivel: My feelings exactly.

The Long Road of the Resistance Movement

Ikeda: I would like to begin by reviewing your human rights struggle.

In an interview, you once explained the personal philosophical background of your participation in the human rights movement.

First, you said your activism derived from your Christian faith. Second, it came from an awareness of the reality, the needs of the people.

And then, in words that I find unforgettable, you said that, coming from a poor family yourself, you had direct personal experience of the poverty of the people, which motivated you to rise up to make a responsible contribution to the people's movement.[2]

I have heard that, born into a poor fishing family, in your youth you sometimes had food one day then went without for three. Experiencing such a life, you saw that poor people often lack the will to demand their just human rights. I understand that when you were twelve or thirteen you decided to get involved in the struggle for human rights by joining Christian groups and populist organizations.

My family produced *nori* (edible seaweed) products, so we, too, made our living from the sea.

When I was in the second year of primary school, my father became bedridden with rheumatism. This made our situation much worse, but my mother kept her spirits up and often joked that though we might be poor, we were "champion-class poor people."

In an air raid during World War II, our house was completely destroyed. My brother and I managed to pull a large chest from the fire. Opening it, we found that it contained my younger sister's traditional Girls' Day dolls. My mother encouraged us, saying:

"Someday, we'll be able to live in a fine house where we can display these dolls again."

Her good cheer, optimism, and refusal to accept defeat in times of trouble illuminated our hearts with the light of hope.

People's lives were incredibly hard in those days. But in any age, the people possess great inner strength and resilience. Battling against adversity, they manage to live out their lives with perseverance, wishing for peace, finding hope, and seeking happiness. That is why we must never lose sight of the great rule: no matter what the situation, fight for the people, communicate with the people, and die with the people.

Esquivel: That is absolutely true. When people work together for the shared objectives of liberty and peace, they can demonstrate extraordinary capabilities. In the early 1970s, as I was busily organizing the Peace and Justice Service (Servicio de Paz y Justicia, SERPAJ) in Latin America, I traveled to different countries, where I met with religious and ecclesiastical communities, agricultural and indigenous leaders, educators' unions, and representatives of the very poorest sectors of the population.

In spite of their own poverty, many of the men and women I met were able to come together and share their own bread with the needy. This really marvelous experience reconciled us to the capacity of the poor for social, cultural, and spiritual resistance. It rewarded us greatly with strength and hope.

In all parts of Latin America, even in isolated and inhospitable places, we encountered men and women who shared their lives with the people and worked to find ways and alternatives to solve the problems they faced. Many of them had sacrificed their lives for the people.

Ikeda: That is deeply moving testimony. It makes me wish to put my palms together in a gesture of reverence to their dedication. As you say, when people have dedicated their lives to a great purpose, they can tap immeasurable powers.

With the slogan of "Struggle through Nonviolence," SERPAJ became active in expanding a people's network throughout all parts of Latin America.

Esquivel: That is correct. It spread throughout Latin America as social resistance and popular struggles took place all over the continent. It was a long struggle.

The Brutality of State Terrorism

Esquivel: A shocking event occurred in 1973, the year before we founded SERPAJ. General Augusto Pinochet (1915–2006) carried out a military coup in Chile. The coup had the support of the Nixon administration in the United States, with Henry Kissinger as the Secretary of State.

Pinochet established a military dictatorship. The human cost to the Chilean people was tremendous. It destroyed the productive capacity of the country and imposed state terrorism on Chilean society. Countless individuals were abducted and "disappeared," and there were shootings, acts of torture, and mass imprisonment. Thousands of Chileans fled their country and went into exile.

We received some of these exiles in Buenos Aires and helped them and their families travel to safety abroad.

Ikeda: Former Chilean president Patricio Aylwin Azócar (1918–2016) told me much about the abuse of human rights by the Pinochet militarist regime. President Aylwin is known as the leader who fought against Pinochet's military dictatorship and eventually effected the transition to a civilian government. He has said:

The military government led by General Pinochet was a dictatorship characterized by implacable harshness, especially in its first years. Tens of thousands were arrested, relocated, or exiled[3] . . .

More than two thousand people were shot without trial or under convictions in summary military trials. More than a thousand were declared missing, which means they were killed and their bodies dumped into the sea or buried in places where no one could find them.[4]

President Aylwin described the situation with the words "An empire of fear was imposed on Chile."[5] In that period, rule by fear spread to all parts of Latin America.

Esquivel: Unfortunately, it did. For years we worked in countries where untold horrors and serious human rights violations were part of the very fabric of the lives of the people. Such occurrences took place practically every day under the military dictatorships of Chile, Brazil, Paraguay, Bolivia, Uruguay, and Guatemala.

In the four countries of Ecuador, Brazil, Chile, and Uruguay, some Latin American bishops and I were arrested and expelled to other nations by the ruling dictatorships. We lodged complaints with the Organization of American States, the European Parliament, the United Nations, and other international organizations. Though only a few doors were opened to us, we knew that saving lives depended on our efforts. We helped relocate political refugees mainly to Canada, Sweden, and other European nations.

The Archives of Terror, discovered in Asunción, Paraguay, proved the existence of what was called Operation Condor. These files revealed the division of roles and responsibilities of the "implementation" squads who were assassinating, abducting, and transferring prisoners from one country to another when intervening in other Latin American countries. We referred to Operation Condor as Terror International (*La Internacional del Terror*).

The squads responsible for implementing the program were paramilitary or para-police. Their operations extended beyond Latin America to the United States and Europe.

Ikeda: Operation Condor revealed how the militaries in various Latin American countries exchanged information about people opposed to them and cooperated in arresting and transferring them to other countries. They abducted refugees and secretly sent them back to the regimes they were fleeing, then publicly declared that they had "disappeared." These are some of the criminal acts in which they were implicated, to my knowledge.

The forces of evil are quick to collude. The forces for good, on the other hand, rarely unite. This is one of the factors accounting for much of the tragedy of the past. Unifying the forces for good is surely the key to a brighter future and the only way to resist evil comprehensively.

Esquivel: That's right. At first our efforts were very weak, but as we went along, we discovered that our weakness was actually a source of strength. We had to learn a great deal before we realized that.

We had to have faith in the will of God, the power of prayer and reflection, our power to resist, and in each of us. We had to cultivate inner strength so that fear did not dominate us.

One of the most gratifying developments in our experiences was the growth of an ecumenism, transcending ideological and sectarian barriers, among diverse Christian and non-Christian groups acting together for the people.

This ecumenism without barriers, united in defense of the life and dignity of the people, emerged from the needs of the public.

Many agnostics also took part. Though without religious beliefs, they identified with the social need for religion and on many occasions participated in prayer and meditation meetings, offering suggestions with the single goal in mind of saving lives.

This encouraged us to continue the struggle.

Ikeda: The ecumenism you speak of is extremely important. It reminds me of something my mentor Josei Toda (1900–58), second president of the Soka Gakkai, frequently said:

If such philosophical and religious giants as Nichiren, Shakyamuni, Jesus Christ, Mohammed, Marx, and others could come together for a conference, their discussion would be informed by a spirit of great compassion and characterized by mutual deference, respect, and reflection. As a means to achieving the fundamental goal of the eternal happiness of humanity, they would no doubt agree completely on the need to bring an end to war, violence, and conflict, and lead humanity to true peace and prosperity.

Only by returning to the original spirit of these great founders of religions and philosophies—the question, "How can we save those who are troubled, suffering, and ill in the real world?"—can we find a way forward that avoids the pitfalls of intolerant radicalism and conflict.

The true purpose of religion is the happiness of human beings, not religion for religion's sake. From the perspective of this essential humanistic mission of religion, all religions should be able to overcome their differences and work together for the welfare of the human race and for peace.

Violence Is the Law of Brutes, Nonviolence the Law of Humankind

Ikeda: The struggle against military dictatorships is a life-and-death battle.

Esquivel: We were well aware of the dangers we faced. We also knew that those threats extended to all activists, including the members of SERPAJ and their family members.

I recall the great teacher and spiritual leader Mahatma Gandhi (1869–1948) said that fear paralyzes, and it is only a step from fear to cowardice.

I have often reflected on this observation. If we allow ourselves to be defeated by cowardice, we lose the fundamental condition of our humanity and are transformed into objects subject to the domineering authoritarianism that generates violence and fear.

Ikeda: That is a valuable and important testament. In your courageous nonviolent activities, you have manifested the true strength of the human spirit.

As an absolutely committed practitioner of nonviolence, Gandhi wrote: "Non-violence is the law of our species as violence is the law of the brute. The spirit lies dormant in the brute and he knows no law but that of physical might. The dignity of man requires obedience to a higher law—to the strength of the spirit."[6]

As Gandhi observes, violence is the explosion of brutishness, and nonviolence is the manifestation of the indomitable human spirit. Nonviolence is the proof of our humanity.

While you and your associates were working together for human rights, the threat of militarism was spreading throughout Latin America. For instance, from the 1950s, political power changed hands time and time again between militaristic and democratic regimes in your own homeland of Argentina. In 1973, Juan Domingo Perón (1895–1974) became president for the third time. Upon his death, his wife, Isabel, became president, and the political situation worsened.

Esquivel: The general crisis broke out in 1975. Many individuals— men and women, young and old—rushed to our Latin America branch of SERPAJ for help in finding loved ones and friends who had gone missing. We heard their heart-rending cries.

But the state remained silent, or simply repeated its denials. Most churches shut their doors on victims' families. Labor unions and political parties had been neutralized, too. So relatives came to us with their grief.

We announced our solidarity with their efforts. Sharing their pain, we took their part and made a solid effort to help them. Of course, simply listening passively was insufficient. It was necessary to take action.

Our consciences, spirits, and human dignity would not permit us to remain indifferent to the suffering of our people.

Ikeda: Indifference to the suffering of others represents our failure as human beings, while the victory of humanity is to be found in empathizing and acting for the benefit of others.

In the *Republic,* the great philosopher Plato (427–347 BCE) sharply rebukes as cowards those who think only of themselves and turn away from social realities. Such a person, he says, "will keep quiet, and mind his own business, like someone taking shelter behind a wall when he is caught by a storm of driving dust and rain. He sees everyone else brimful of lawlessness, and counts himself lucky if he himself can somehow live his life here pure, free from injustice and unholy actions."[7]

But that is not the way to change society, and through such behavior one's own spirit is consumed by evil.

Tsunesaburo Makiguchi (1871–1944), first president of the Soka Gakkai, warned: "Failing to do good is equivalent to doing evil in terms of the consequences of one's actions."[8] Doing nothing allows evil to run rampant and prevail. It is therefore tantamount to doing evil oneself.

Burning with the flame of justice, Dr. Esquivel, you risked your life to fight against evil—for the sake of the people. Realizing that, the people must heartily praise and support you.

Esquivel: As your quotation from the *Republic* indicates, human beings are compelled to choose their path.

Do we close our ears, eyes, and hearts to the people around us and go our own ways as if they were of no importance? This is to choose egoism, to choose barricading ourselves up in our own small shell of selfishness. That is one way to live one's life.

Or we can make our way through life with the people and our comrades, sharing one another's sufferings. That is another way of life. The paths we choose are decisive in defining our life.

We were incapable of remaining indifferent in the face of the people's suffering.

Lies as the Instrument of Violence

Ikeda: On the subject of human suffering, Argentina experienced a period of social turbulence and unrest from the late 1960s into the 1970s.

This was related not only to tensions resulting from complex political and economic circumstances unique to Argentina but also various regional and international developments that impacted Latin America. In these circumstances, General Jorge Videla (1925–2013) led a coup d'état that removed Isabel Perón from office.

Esquivel: The coup took place on March 24, 1976, and the armed forces assumed total power.

During this period, the so-called National Security Doctrine reached its apogee on the South American continent. People were kidnapped and "disappeared," and the state was intent on evading its responsibility toward them. Since judicial protection no longer functioned, the people were left completely vulnerable.

Under such conditions, we could not remain indifferent. We were compelled to muster our forces and try to denounce injustices. Our basic task was reclaiming from the government the rights of individuals and of the people as a whole.

Ikeda: Under the military dictatorship (1976–83), many precious Argentine lives were lost at the hands of the military government and its security forces.

During this period, you boldly rose up to do something about the situation. In June 1994, to an assembly of spellbound Soka University students, you related experiences from this dark period: "Of course, all thirty thousand were not killed at once. They disappeared one or two at a time. Though the number of victims rose to five, ten, one hundred, there was no cry of protest from society. And that is why thirty thousand people lost their lives."[9]

The students listened to your account of these events, too shocking to be imagined by anyone who had not actually survived them.

Those considered undesirable by the military government were made to "disappear" quietly, one at a time. And then the government lied, saying that it had nothing to do with the disappearances.

In your writings, you have revealed the truth and vehemently denounced the government's deliberate policy to make large numbers of completely innocent individuals "disappear."

The majority of the mass media bought the authorities' attempts to smear the victims as villains, even though they were completely innocent. As a result, the general public, who did not know the individuals involved, were convinced of the government's claims.

Esquivel: Unfortunately, that is true.

Ikeda: The great French writer Victor Hugo (1802–85) once wrote that "lying is the very face of the Devil."[10]

The constant repetition of lies deceives the people into believing falsehoods to be true and injustices to be just. This is the standard practice adopted by evil. Cowardly lies are the companions of violence.

That is why the just must never remain silent. Justice is not real unless it speaks out with the voice of truth.

While many people preferred to remain silent and uninvolved, you, on the other hand, were unable to keep still in the attempt of the authorities to shut down people's consciences. You fought at the frontlines to give voice to those suffering from oppression, those denied of their voices.

Esquivel: As Christians, we were responsible for our neighbors, our people, and other peoples of the world.

There are common values that identify us as members of the greater human family.

Ikeda: I agree. We need to willingly shoulder responsibility for other people and society. We need to act altruistically. This true religious spirit is the source for elevating, fortifying, and expanding the soul.

One of the important factors required in a religion for the twenty-first century is that it makes a contribution to humanity.

Buddhism teaches the model of the bodhisattva—a life dedicated to true self-realization for both oneself and all other beings. It is an ideal of an awakened individual who bears a heavy responsibility for the happiness of all beings. Bodhisattvas affirm their responsibility for all living beings in the form of "four universal vows."

The first is the vow to save innumerable living beings. This is a vow to aid all suffering beings throughout their lives.

The second is the vow to eradicate countless earthly desires. This is the vow to confront the earthly desires, or the base impulses inherent in life, and transform each and every one into enlightenment.

The third vow is to master immeasurable Buddhist teachings. Today, by extension the term "Buddhist teachings" can include all the philosophies and systems of thought produced by human beings throughout history. It is the vow to study, based on Buddhism, the full spiritual and intellectual heritage of the human race and put it to use to aid living beings.

The fourth vow—to attain supreme enlightenment—is the vow to attain the self-perfection taught by Buddhism. It means becoming one with the fundamental and the eternal, and establishing the Greater Self.

In other words, the bodhisattva represents a life dedicated to true self-realization for both oneself and all other beings. It is an ideal of an awakened individual who bears a heavy responsibility for the happiness of all beings. The four universal vows represent the conviction that the struggle to aid the people is the greatest value human beings can create.

To make the dignity of human life shine its brightest, the bodhisattva strives to meet the challenge of the "great good" of aiding the people. No matter how difficult the circumstances, the bodhisattva acts to create value. The Japanese word for creating value, *soka,* is part of the name of the Soka Gakkai.

Esquivel: Value creation—*soka*—is what motivates the will to fight for dignity, the values that make us human, and the societies we are trying to construct. This will to fight emerges from our faith and commitment to life. The search for points of consensus among religions through interfaith dialogue enables us to discover fresh perspectives and ideas for analyzing our situation and understanding the human condition in all its complexity, the life of the people, and the ways of power.

Ikeda: I agree. When the military coup d'état took place in Argentina, you had already been actively engaged in the struggle against the suppression of human rights in many parts of Latin America.

As is well known, you were in the forefront of the march of the Mothers of the May Plaza (Madres de Plaza de Mayo), working in solidarity with families demanding the return of vanished loved ones.

Choosing a Life of Difficult Struggle

Ikeda: Your family is very artistic. You are a sculptor, painter, and architect, and your wife, Amanda, is a pianist and composer.

Esquivel: Certainly our lives as artists and teachers have been good and successful.

Amanda has appeared in piano concerts and composes in different forms, including symphonies, chorales, cantatas, and quartets. I have held exhibitions, produced monuments, and taught on the Faculty of Architecture and Urbanism of the Universidad Nacional de la Plata, in art schools, and at the Instituto del Profesorado. I have also taught at a teacher's college training secondary school teachers. All the while our little children were growing up and enjoying their lives.

Ikeda: If you and your wife had chosen, as a sculptor and a musician, to live lives dedicated solely to art, your lives may well have been quiet and peaceful. Yet you chose the turbulent life of the struggle for human rights. You chose to help the unfortunate. I would like to offer you my highest praises for making that choice.

In art or religion, nothing is more comfortable than remaining within one's personal comfort zone and ignoring the suffering in society. Such a life is free of criticism and pressure. But you have braved tempestuous adversity to join the people and work for their interests.

In that mighty struggle you became a sculptor of supreme character, an architect of an immortal life, and your wife a composer of eternal humanity.

Esquivel: Thank you very much for your understanding and recognition.

I always consider myself a laborer, a patient artisan modeling forms that emerge from my hands and tools.

Not all my materials are equal. Each has its own energy, its emerging vitality that I must liberate so that it can become fully alive. It is also necessary to discover and respect the essential character of the material.

Ikeda: Every one of your words powerfully conveys your stubborn resistance to evil and the passion that compels you to help the suffering. Identifying yourself as a laborer reveals awareness of yourself as a human being free of any form of pretense or affectation. It shines with the pride of walking arm in arm with the people, which was also Mahatma Gandhi's spirit.

Dedicating one's life to fighting for others, whatever the cost—this noble ideal is the spirit of the bodhisattva taught in Buddhism.

In your struggles, not only you but your son was arrested.

Esquivel: That's right, in May 1976. The police raided the offices of SERPAJ and arrested all our associates, including my oldest son, Leonardo.

At the time, Amanda and I were in Vienna working with various organizations and denouncing serious human rights violations in Argentina and other South American countries. We immediately initiated an international campaign and succeeded in having our associates liberated in two days.

As a result of this incident, we therefore decided to get our children out of the country. The Austrian embassy in Argentina protected them and succeeded in getting them out. After meeting up with our children in Geneva, we took refuge in Vienna. Then after traveling to Brussels, we decided to go to Paris.

We had many sympathetic friends in Europe and could have settled there. But my work and commitment were with my people and my fellow Argentinians and Latin Americans. I could not leave my compatriots exposed to the hazards represented by the military dictatorship. With great courage and sense of purpose, they resolved not to close SERPAJ but to continue working at the risk of everything.

Ikeda: You and your family were true comrades to your compatriots at SERPAJ, and you could not betray them. You chose the path of integrity and virtue.

As you continued the battle in the name of the peoples of Latin America, the oppression of the authorities against you intensified.

The Courage of a Woman When Her Husband Was Arrested

Esquivel: Yes, it did.

I traveled to Ecuador, where I was arrested. While taking part in a conference of Latin American bishops in Ecuador, I was arrested in Riobamba, at the Casa de la Santa Cruz, and imprisoned. Arrested with me were seventeen Latin American bishops and four lay and religious North Americans.

When finally I was released, I discussed the matter with my family, and we decided to return to Argentina. We could not abandon our comrades and people. We had to give testimony and set an example in both struggle and resistance.

We all knew the possible consequences of our actions. Amanda's great firmness and courage were a mainstay. With her great resolution, she always demonstrates calm and equilibrium.

With my family I returned to Argentina, where, as I was trying to renew my passport, the Central Department of Federal Police detained me.

Ikeda: I believe that was in April 1977. Falsely accused of crimes, and without due process of law, you were incarcerated in Buenos Aires.

I have heard that you were subjected to harsh torture, including electrical shocks. It was a time when the situation was growing darker and darker for dissidents, who never knew when they might be killed.

Your arrest was completely unexpected. As you said, you had gone to renew your passport, and the authorities suddenly arrested you without giving any reason. When your wife, learning of your fate, hurried to the prison, the authorities lied to her, saying that you had not been arrested and that you were not there. Their malevolent intent was to quietly eradicate someone they considered a troublemaker.

You owed your life to the courageous acts of your wife.

For a few days, newspapers reported your disappearance. But your wife refused to go away silently. Accompanied by lawyers, she went to the authorities and insisted that you had been arrested while the two of you were renewing your passports. In fact, she hadn't actually been with you at the time, but saying this helped give credence to her insistence that you had been arrested.

When the truth became public knowledge, the authorities could no longer silence you. Your wife displayed enormous courage and wisdom.

Esquivel: Indeed, that is absolutely true.

I knew the authorities were looking for me, but I had nothing to hide. Our work was always within the law and perfectly legitimate.

But the military had other ideas.

After I was detained, Amanda courageously hurried to the police department, where she announced that she knew where I was and wanted to see me.

First they denied that I was being held in the Federal Security Supervision Prison. But Amanda insisted that she knew different because she was there with me when I was detained. Finally, her firmness and resolution were so strong that the police had to admit they had lied about my detention. This was the beginning of our long struggle against the military government.

Struggling against Harsh Prison Conditions

Ikeda: The faces of you and your wife shine with the indomitable fighting spirit of a couple who have united in choosing a life of turbulent struggle for their beliefs. When I met your wife, I saw her sitting quietly beside you with a smile. I am convinced that your drama of victory is hers as well.

Esquivel: I am wholeheartedly grateful to her both as a wife and as a comrade.

She knocked on the doors of many ministries and churches, just like the women who later formed the Mothers of May Plaza movement. She visited bishops, ambassadors, and various organizations for both my liberation and the liberation of others kidnapped or missing. Most of the doors she knocked on remained firmly closed. People wanted to find a way to shirk any responsibility.

Out of fear, many of our friends would not so much as telephone us.

At about that time, delegations, international jurists, and representatives of churches and human rights organizations began coming to Argentina. Unyielding in the face of government pressure and threats, they held conferences and started resistance movements.

When she was finally allowed to see me, Amanda told me of the things being done by organizations and the joint actions of many countries around the world for the sake of my freedom.

Ikeda: Your fourteen months in prison (until June 1978) must have been indescribably bitter.

I believe I know from experience—albeit a brief one—what you must have felt.

I was imprisoned on false charges[11] during the hottest days of summer in 1957, in an attempt by the authorities to stop the Soka Gakkai's people's movement. I was put in a tiny solitary cell with barred windows. The temperatures in the cell soared to over 40 degrees Celsius, day after day. I remember that I slept leaning on the wall, which was slightly cooler than the rest of the room.

Prosecutors threatened to arrest Mr. Toda unless I admitted to the charges brought against me. It was not until four and a half years later that I was finally cleared in a court of law.

Esquivel: I see. I am certain that, as an educator and a person of awakened conscience, you understand what I say.

Ikeda: The inherent violence of authority is starkly revealed in prison. Only people who have experienced imprisonment can know how fearsome it is.

I understand that your solitary cell was barely four paces from side to side. Broken windows let in the cold, making sleep difficult—in addition to which your jailor woke you every two hours.

The aim, no doubt, was to break you physically and mentally. But you endured it all triumphantly.

Esquivel: For the first days of my imprisonment, I was shut up in a solitary cell called a *tubo*. In that tiny, nauseating space, the time passed monotonously, with no distinction between day and night.

The only sounds were those of the transfer of prisoners and the racket of weapons and vehicles. Amanda came every day to bring me food and sometimes was allowed to spend a few minutes with me.

When the *tubo* was opened, the bright light of the outside corridor dazzled me, and I felt dizzy until my eyes became accustomed to it. I was able to see many inscriptions made by former inmates held in the cell while they were being tortured.

There were prayers and names of loved ones. I even remember some of them today.

"In the twilight of life, you will be reclaimed in love."

"Father, forgive them, for they know not what they do."

"God save us and grant us Your peace."

I remember also insults directed toward the police and the military and the names and emblems of favorite soccer clubs.

But the one that made the most profound mental and spiritual impression on me was a large stain on a cell wall. Little by little, it became apparent that the stain was blood, in which someone had written, "God does not kill."

This was the cry from the soul of someone driven to an extreme state by torment, the proof of her or his faith. Even in that horrible situation, the person was able to invoke God with his or her own blood.

Ikeda: It is a cry that can never be forgotten.

Esquivel: In prison, we were repeatedly tortured and humiliated. Many were destroyed physically and spiritually, reduced to a dehumanized state. They lost the power to resist and all sense of meaning in life. They were crushed.

Others, including myself, learned how to keep from being crushed, how not to submit.

It is not that we were better or stronger. In my own case, I believe that what sustained me and gave me the power of spiritual resistance was that I knew that liberty cannot be incarcerated in any prison, that it lives inside us. Freedom lives in commitment, in the decision to take the people's part, and in knowing that you are not alone, that many men, women, organizations, and religious groups were with us, joining us in prayer and struggle.

This encouraged my prison companions and me.

Resistance was our byword.

The Struggle against Japan's Military Government

Ikeda: "Liberty lives inside us"—only someone who has walked the line between life and death could utter those golden words. They demonstrate the formidable power of your spirit.

Nichiren (1222–82), whose Buddhism members of the SGI follow, spent his life fighting against persecution by the authorities, yet he declared: "Even if it seems that, because I was born in the ruler's domain, I follow him in my actions, I will never follow him in my heart."[12]

He spoke these words to one of the most influential government officials of his day, Hei no Saemon-no-jo (d. 1293), after returning to the city of Kamakura, the political center of the country at the time, from unjust exile on the Island of Sado.

This declaration is an encapsulation of the spirit he demonstrated throughout life. It is also the essence of Buddhism and the main current of the SGI struggle for human rights.

Nichiren's words, like the roar of a lion, are included in the chapter "Limitations on Power" in the important human rights work *Birthright of Man: An Anthology of Texts on Human Rights,* published in 1969 by UNESCO to commemorate the twentieth anniversary of the adoption of the Universal Declaration of Human Rights.

The first two Soka Gakkai presidents, Makiguchi and Toda, inherited Nichiren's unyielding spirit. Even during the days of fanatic Japanese nationalism preceding World War II, they boldly spoke out for true Buddhism and unceasingly struggled in the name of peace and the happiness of the people.

Nichiren also battled against the Kamakura government, which was a military regime, and the struggle of the first two Soka Gakkai presidents was also a struggle against a military dictatorship. Their freedom of speech was restricted, and they were subjected to surveillance and harassment by the Special Higher Police, a kind of "thought police." Eventually, they were wrongfully arrested and imprisoned.

Although he had no great understanding of Buddhism, Makiguchi's contemporary and the father of Japanese folklore studies Kunio Yanagita (1875–1962), reminiscing about Makiguchi after the war, wrote:

> Working with young people, he proclaimed doctrines of pacifism and opposition to the war. For this reason, the military frowned upon him and ultimately senselessly imprisoned him. He refused to make the concessions his captors required and died either in prison or immediately after being released. In other words, he suffered the kind of martyrdom not uncommon in the history of religious founders.[13]

In spite of undergoing harsh interrogation at the hands of the Special Higher Police, Makiguchi refused to retreat from his convictions.

Japan at that time had adopted State Shinto as its spiritual pillar and regarded itself as "the Land of the Gods." The government had labeled their war of aggression a "holy war," a claim which Makiguchi rejected absolutely. In the transcripts of his interrogations by the Special Higher Police, we find him quoted as saying: "Japan's slander of the Law is the real cause of the present Sino-Japanese War and the Greater East Asian War [namely, World War II]."[14]

The militarist government of the time employed the idea of a holy war to rally the populace, and, under the rubric of creating "The Greater East Asia Co-Prosperity Sphere," justified their invasions of China and numerous other Asian nations. Makiguchi, however, utterly and completely rejected this spiritual foundation for the war.

The "Law" referred to in the phrase "slander of the Law" employed by Makiguchi is the teaching in the Lotus Sutra of the sanctity and dignity of life. Asserting that Japan had slandered, or rejected, the idea of the sanctity of life and was ruthlessly violating that principle through the brutality of its wars of invasion, Makiguchi denounced the war as slander of the Law. Remaining faithful to his religious convictions, he fought against his nation that was slandering the Law, and was imprisoned as a result.

But even though subjected to the harsh conditions of imprisonment, Makiguchi serenely proclaimed that his hardships were "infinitesimally small" when compared to the momentous persecutions suffered by Nichiren.

Even though the elderly Makiguchi was confined to a cold, dark, cramped solitary cell, his mind was focused on the future of his society and the people, until at last he died in prison.

His disciple Toda was eventually released from prison and pledged to see his mentor and his struggle against the militarist authorities vindicated. With the vow to be an indomitable champion comparable to the Count of Monte Cristo in the famous novel by Alexandre Dumas (1802–70), he rose up after the war dedicated to building a society of peace and human rights. I shall always remember hearing him echo his mentor's words by saying, in a choked voice, that his own sufferings were insignificant in comparison with those of Makiguchi.

Fortified by Imprisonment

Esquivel: I am greatly impressed and gratified to hear of the struggle of the first three Soka Gakkai presidents, and feel profound sympathy with the words of Nichiren you have shared with me.

Nichiren's statements are very clear: life is worth living only when liberty breathes in truth and in light-dispelling darkness.

This value system reminds me of the idea that values are the means for reconciling us with life.

The lotus of the Lotus Sutra rises from the mud to bloom in undefiled glory. In other words, it symbolizes a light transcending the phenomenal world and illuminating the true essence of reality.

Ikeda: In 1944, while still in prison, Toda read the Lotus Sutra repeatedly, eventually awakening to the profound conviction that "the Buddha is life itself." This was the realization that the Buddha exists both within ourselves and throughout the universe. It is the fundamental life force of the universe.

The Buddha as taught in the Lotus Sutra is the life force that exists in the depths of all people's lives. At the same time, this life force transcends the individual and pervades all things and all phenomena in the universe.

Having profoundly apprehended the life of Buddha in both himself and all people living in this corrupt and defiled world—rife with violence, war, conflict, discrimination, the suppression of human rights, and environmental destruction, Toda developed the idea of the human revolution and started a movement dedicated to leading people to enlightenment. This spiritual leap he made while still in prison became a major driving force in the later development of the Soka Gakkai.

Esquivel: I am certain that your mentors' commitment and service to their people and to all humanity were not in vain and have borne fruit that are multiplying in the world today.

Ikeda: I deeply appreciate your reassuring assessment.

The first prime minister of independent India, Jawaharlal Nehru (1889–1964), who was imprisoned nine times, said: "Prison affects people in various ways; some break down or weaken, others grow harder and more confirmed in their convictions, and it is usually the latter whose influence is felt more by the mass of the people."[15]

Without a doubt, you belong to that latter category, Dr. Esquivel.

Esquivel: You praise me too highly.

Ikeda: For the sake of future generations, I would like to ask you further about your experience in prison.

Esquivel: Certainly. In prison, when night fell and the guards had gone, closing the barred cell doors, I had about an hour for exercise and yoga. This was my only time for it, since we were forbidden exercise. If I had been caught at it, I would have been taken to the torture house.

Meditation was fundamental for me. I strove to attend to two things: what took place within me and what took place outside me. I wanted to attain interior equilibrium, in which to hear the silence of God.

"Death Flight"—Being Dropped from a Plane

Ikeda: For you, just surviving each day was an arduous struggle.

I have heard that in one instance, you were placed in a situation on the verge of death.

Esquivel: Yes, that's true. It happened at sunrise on May 5, 1977. I was taken from prison and, still fettered, was driven in a patrol car to San Justo Airport. I was forced on a plane and chained to one of the seats in the rear. Thus began what I thought would be my death flight.

For two hours, or perhaps longer, we flew over the Río de la Plata and the sea. The idea that I was about to be thrown out into the sea raced through my mind, and for a moment I was overcome with terror, but I nonetheless tried to calm my spirit and heart through prayer.

Ikeda: It was an extreme situation when you felt as if you could see your own death. What was going on inside the plane?

Esquivel: Onboard were the murderous guards. They were waiting to commit another crime to add to their terrible list of crimes. To such slaves to violence, their human victims are invisible.

They were preparing to throw me into the Río de la Plata or the sea. As I watched them, I wondered how many people they had thrown into the sea alive. I asked myself how they managed to keep a serene conscience and, after finishing the assassination, return home to love their wives and children.

I prayed for the butchers about to kill me. I prayed that in His infinite mercy, God would touch their hearts and pardon them.

I knew the fates of prisoners who, drugged and bound in wires or chains, were tossed into the sea, because at the International Commission of Jurists in Geneva, I had seen microfilms of cadavers washed ashore by currents on the Uruguay coast and of others eaten away by fish.

I felt defenseless and impotent in the face of this mad state in which the human being is considered no more than a disposable object. I could only pray to God for my family, for the people of Argentina and the rest of Latin America, and for myself. I could only ask Him to forgive my faults and to help the people transcend their grave predicament.

Ikeda: You were prepared to die.

Esquivel: The day was cold; the sky was clear and cloudless. The immense serenity of creation enveloped the dawn. I saw the sun rising on the horizon as the sky went red, violet, yellow, and orange. I could not help admiring such beauty, even as hatred and fear filled the plane.

I took a deep breath, perhaps my last. And I gave thanks to God for the chance to behold the great beauty of creation.

Just as preparations for dumping me overboard had been completed, the pilot unexpectedly received orders to take me to the airbase at Morón. The men on board looked at each other either confused by the instructions or disgruntled at being unable to complete their task. The plane headed for the Morón Air Base. There, after some hours of deliberation among the commanders, it was decided to send me to Unit 9 at La Plata, a maximum-security prison.

Ikeda: Why were the orders suddenly changed?

Esquivel: An official told me, "Set your mind at ease. We're taking you to U9. You're safe. You've stirred up a lot of reaction."

On the border between life and death, many things passed through my mind. I lost the capacity to think rationally. Prayer and faith in God were all that sustained me.

Ikeda: The desperate efforts on the part of your wife, Amanda, and many representatives of the ordinary people brought about a sudden reversal of the orders to kill you.

Later, Amnesty International designated you a prisoner of conscience, and many people from around the world sent letters to the Argentine government calling for your release. Then finally in June 1978 you were set free.

Esquivel: Yes, that's correct.

Accepting a Grassroots Nobel Peace Prize as a Representative of the People

Ikeda: For your great achievements as a warrior for human rights and a victor over oppression, you received the Nobel Peace Prize in 1980.

I understand that the fact that you were still in prison when you were nominated was a topic of special interest.

Esquivel: It was indeed. One day Amanda and our son Leonardo came to see me in prison and told me that my nomination for the Nobel Peace Prize was being discussed on the international scene. I had been recommended by Betty Williams (1943–2020) and Mairead Corrigan, Peace Prize laureates from Northern Ireland.

Some months before, I was informed that the organization Pax Christi International had awarded me the Pope John XXIII Peace Memorial Prize.

But all of this seemed remote and strange to me in prison.

Prison is a completely distinct world. Life in a cell is monotonous; punishment is the only alteration in the routine. For prisoners, surviving is the main thing.

Ikeda: You did survive, and were eventually released and renewed your activism.

Two years later, you received notification of having been given the Peace Prize.

Esquivel: I was away from home and when I telephoned my wife, at home, she told me that she had received a telephone call from the Norwegian Embassy and that they urgently wanted to get in touch with me. I headed there at once.

At that time I was providing information on human rights violations to various embassies, and I thought it had something to do with that.

When I arrived, the ambassador informed me that I had been awarded the Nobel Peace Prize. I was more surprised than anybody. I could not believe it was real. There were many candidates who did extraordinary work in many countries—people famous all over the world.

Ikeda: At the time, your Nobel Prize became famous far and wide as the Grassroots Peace Prize. Not long thereafter, the military government issued a statement about patching things up. In it, they mentioned that the news of your Peace Prize had astonished the public in Argentina.

Esquivel: I immediately made it clear that I was not accepting the Nobel Prize as an individual, and that what I had done was not accomplished alone. It was the result of my joint struggle with thousands of men and women—indigenous people, social and religious organizations, and ordinary citizens unaffiliated with any groups or organizations—who shared our struggles, hopes, and hardships, and I could only accept the prize in their name.

I accepted it in the name of the many who work, live, and walk with some of the poorest and most marginalized people on the continent. During the more than twenty years that have passed since

I received the prize (in 1980), I have always tried to keep my words and deeds consistent.

Ikeda: The truly great are truly modest as well. I had the honor of meeting Betty Williams, whom you mentioned earlier, in Tokyo (November 2006), and she was also a genuinely modest and very warm-hearted person.

The bestowal of the Nobel Prize on you, I believe, while a great honor for you, actually enhances the prestige of the prize even more so.

But the Nobel Peace Prize, which you received in the very midst of your struggles, was by no means your final destination as a man who was shouldering the mission of acting to build peace. Since receiving it, you have carried on your struggle in the name of a just society and respect for humanity with even greater energy.

You are still taking part in the search for people arrested and lost without trace under the Argentine military regime.

In cooperation with other Nobel laureates, you have worked to promote global human rights movements and to organize a summit[16] to deliberate on the economies and development problems of industrializing nations while exerting your utmost to eradicate social evil from the world.

Surviving Life-Threatening Crises

Ikeda: Hearing your experiences renews my awareness of the evil inherent in power. Throughout history, it has persecuted countless good individuals and harmed so many innocent people.

As Plato points out in the *Gorgias,* "The very bad men come from the class of those who have power."[17]

The evil of power makes those who wield it reduce other people to tools for the satisfaction of their own desires and take pleasure in subjugating them to their will. In Buddhist terms, this is symbolized by the so-called devil king of the sixth heaven, who envies, hates, reviles, and oppresses followers of true philosophies and religions.

Nichiren too faced life-threatening persecutions on numerous occasions. One of the most perilous was the Tatsunokuchi Persecution (1271), in which he was falsely accused of being a traitor by the Kamakura military government and taken to a place called Tatsunokuchi on the outskirts of Kamakura to be beheaded.

Late at night, treated as a criminal, Nichiren was placed on a horse and surrounded by military guards. Several of his disciples heard of the danger he was in and hurried to his side. Resolved to share Nichiren's martyrdom, they took his horse's reins.

Just before the attempt to execute Nichiren, one of the disciples said in tears to him: "These are your last moments." Nichiren replied: "You don't understand. What greater joy could there be?"[18] This declaration that there is no greater joy than being persecuted and even dying for the truth is, in my estimation, a demonstration of his supreme victory as a human being.

But, just at the last moment, a "shining object" flashed across the night sky with blinding brightness. Dr. Hideo Hirose, professor emeritus and former director of the astronomical observatory of Tokyo University, has suggested that the object may have been a meteor stream in the region of Aries and Taurus constellations.[19]

The amazed soldiers trembled with fear at this unexpected occurrence. As Nichiren himself recorded, "The executioner fell on his face, his eyes blinded. The soldiers were filled with panic. Some ran off into the distance, some jumped down from their horses and huddled on the ground, while others crouched in their saddles."[20] As a result, the execution was not carried out.

Following the Tatsunokuchi incident, Nichiren was exiled to the Island of Sado, from which it was widely accepted that no one returned alive. There, his enemies constantly sought to kill him, and he lacked sufficient clothing and food. Yet even in those circumstances, he wrote numerous treatises and letters of encouragement to disciples, who were deeply disturbed by their teacher's persecution.

As a Buddhist, I believe that the supreme embodiment of our humanity is to never give up, even when facing a life-threatening crisis, to fight against our destiny and change it. The more that thinking and caring people become aware of the depth of the sufferings of our world, the more susceptible they are to despair. That is why I feel it is so important to stress this point.

Destiny Can Be Changed

Esquivel: As you have so eloquently explained, we seem to remain the prisoners of our fate, on a tragic course that cannot be changed.

This calls to mind for me Sisyphus of Greek mythology, who embodies the existential anguish of humanity. For disobedience, Zeus, the supreme Olympian god, condemns Sisyphus to carry a boulder on his shoulders to the pinnacle of a mountain.

Ikeda: It is interesting that you mention Sisyphus. It offers a very vivid image.

Esquivel: The great and strong Sisyphus keeps an eye on his goal as he approaches the top of the mountain step by step. When, exhausted, he is half way up, the stone falls from his back and rolls down to the foot of the mountain. It is his anguishing mission to repeat this task eternally, knowing that all his efforts are futile and that he is condemned to carry on this relentless struggle with his burden through endless time.

Ikeda: Yes, his struggle goes on forever.

Esquivel: Albert Camus (1913–60) called Sisyphus "the Absurd Man,"[21] a hero who attempts the impossible and engages in an endless effort that can never be rewarded. He stands as a symbol of humankind's existential suffering, despair and defeat, and eternal agony.

Like Sisyphus, many members of society today live oppressed by existential anguish: men and women striving in hopelessness and useless heroism and submitting to the fatalistic inevitability of their existence, carrying their own intolerably heavy burdens, without resisting.

But if we look more closely into the lives of the people, we see that they—men and women, young and old, making no pretense to be heroes, day by day are looking for a flower to blossom, a miracle to take place. That flower blossoms in the daily struggle of their lives, in a child's smile, in the creation of hope, and in the illumination of our path showing us that our exertions are our liberation.

Ikeda: That is a splendid way to express it, and just what one would expect from a man such as you, who has lived his life with the people. We must, as you say, ensure that the flower of hope blooms in peoples' lives.

Esquivel: To continue with my earlier paradigm, the instant the stone falls from his shoulders, Sisyphus impotently and sorrowfully beholds his own eternal anguish. As he watches it roll down to the foot of the mountain he knows he is condemned to retrace his steps and recommence the laborious task. Not only must he carry the boulder again, he must tell himself that he must start again.

From a cursory reading of the circumstances humankind faces, of human behavior throughout history, of our wild violence at all times, it would seem that nothing changes. It is as if the human condition were inextricably bound to violence and that all our efforts to overcome it were useless.

Ikeda: Undeniably the pessimistic view that war and violence are such entrenched instincts in human beings that they are ineradicable is deep rooted. Many dismiss the idea of a world without war as a fantasy. But such a fatalistic view only diminishes and delimits our future.

In ancient India, around the time of the establishment of Buddhism, various ideas about human fate were advanced. Some of them resembled views of fate such as those articulated by the Greek concept of the Fates or an existential suffering like that of Sisyphus. In general they fall into three categories.

First is the fatalistic notion that present and future are determined irrevocably by the past. No matter what efforts one makes in the present, one's predetermined fate cannot be changed. In fact, any such effort is itself an expression of one's predetermined fate.

Second is the idea of divine will, the theory of fate as taught by Brahmanism. According to this doctrine, the will of the gods determines the caste and condition into which a person is born. This idea of divine will underlies the prevalence of the discriminative Indian caste system.

Third is the doctrine of chance, which argued that human life is entirely fortuitous, without any specific causes or conditions shaping it. This doctrine of chance teaches that our happiness or misery is unconnected to our behavior, which leads to the rejection of all morals and ethics.

Esquivel: Essentially, our views on fate are profoundly connected to how we respond to our times and our society.

Ikeda: Indian society in Shakyamuni's time was dominated by the doctrines of fatalism and the belief in divine determination. Shakyamuni refuted these views of fate.

For instance, on one occasion, as he was sitting in meditation under a tree, a Brahman approached and, concluding that the meditating man must be of lowly status, asked Shakyamuni about his birth.

Shakyamuni replied: "Do not ask about descent, but ask about conduct. Truly from wood fire is produced. A sage, possessed of firmness, although of lowly birth, becomes a thoroughbred, having modesty as his restraint."[22]

Human beings are not defined by birth or circumstances; it is deeds, not birth, that matter. This idea represented a great awakening and inspiration to those who had given up on life and themselves because they believed their fate was predetermined.

Shakyamuni also taught a philosophy of personal autonomy, asserting that we have the free will to alter our own destiny. Nichiren also wrote, "There are not two lands, pure or impure in themselves. The difference lies solely in the good or evil of our minds."[23]

By an impure land, Nichiren means the world of delusion and ignorance plagued by violence, war, poverty, and oppression. He contrasts this with the pure and tranquil land where the Buddha dwells. This land is filled with joy and wisdom, where nonviolence and peace, equality, freedom, and compassion prevail.

Nichiren argued that it is people's minds—the individual's state of life at any given moment—that determine whether the world is pure or impure. We can transform our world into a pure land by transforming the evil mind making the world impure into a mind of goodness. This is a process leading from the transformation of the individual to the transformation of society. The fight against war and discrimination is carried out by acting based on a network bringing together the goodness in people's hearts, which ignites the light of hope in the people and ensures enduring social change.

You are a true champion of human rights who has tirelessly fought for the sake of humanity and the future. Through your struggle for human rights you have given rise to one of the great transformations in human history. I am certain that the radiant hope you have inspired will continue to expand and illuminate the future of humankind.

TWO

A World United by the Power of the People

The World Seen from Latin America

Ikeda: Construction is a life-and-death struggle, while destruction happens in a moment.

The Argentinian author Eduardo Mallea (1903–82) has written: "What you need, people, what you need are builders; you need builders among the people; the advance created by builders."[1]

You have struggled for many long years as a builder of happiness and peace for the people. In this chapter, I would like to begin by discussing the future of Latin America.

Esquivel: Latin America possesses a great creative capacity and enormous resilience. At the same time, the continent faces great challenges, which can make their appearance at unpredictable moments, carrying its people along a path weaving between successes and failures.

Latin America finds itself in a space between hope and despair.

Ikeda: I am certain Latin America faces many future challenges, but as democracy gains on the continent, it is receiving attention for its economic growth.

As the "B" in the acronym BRICs [Brazil, Russia, India, and China], Brazil is regarded as one of the new emerging economies in the world today. A more recent acronym, VISTA, cites Vietnam, Indonesia, South Africa, Turkey, and Argentina as important growing economies.

At the same time, when Latin America is viewed as a whole, the problems of rising crime rates caused by poverty, deteriorating security, and environmental degradation must be acknowledged. The legacy of the former military dictatorships also represents a heavy burden.

Esquivel: The military dictatorships imposed on Latin America have left a tragic legacy in the forms of the loss of human life and property. The wounds of that past are not yet healed. The huge foreign debts generated by the economic destruction of the period of military rule—debts that they are still carrying—have created a state of chronic economic crisis for many Latin American states.

Ikeda: How can Latin America, existing as you said in the space between hope and despair, climb steadily up the slope of hope? What will be the energy, the springboard for that shift? What obstacles stand in its way, and how can they be overcome?

In the 1980s, often called Latin America's "lost decade," many countries suffered hyperinflation. In 1989, inflation in Argentina reached a rate of 5,000 percent.

In the 1990s, Argentina became a model of economic growth. But in 2001, the economy was once more imperiled, this time by default. Today, as a once-in-a-century economic crisis threatens the world, the lives of many people in Argentina and elsewhere have grown increasingly difficult.

Esquivel: Argentina's accumulated foreign debt—what I call an eternal debt—grew explosively as a result of the economic policies of the military dictatorship.

It is a debt stained with the blood of the people, immoral and illegitimate, generated through the collusion of giant multinational corporations and Argentine businesses. It originated when the dictatorship nationalized the companies responsible and shifted their debt to the Argentine people.

No government in Latin America to this day has undertaken any investigation into which debts are legitimate and which are not. The government of Ecuador is the exception, and is presently conducting such an investigation.

What has been the result of forcing the people to shoulder this enormous debt? A shortage of funds for health, education, and development, and a growing problem with hunger.

In this context, Argentina's foreign debt is not a thing of the past, because it still weighs very heavily on the lives of the people. Material wealth is concentrated in the centers of power, further aggravating the problems of hunger and poverty.

As you noted earlier, we have seen increasing democratization in Latin America, and with the arrival of civilian governments, elections are being held, but the mechanisms of oppression by great economic and political interests still remain front and center. While there are political leaders who pay attention to the wishes of the people and try to respond to them, the old structures and institutions remain in place and continue to act.

What, in fact, has really changed? It can be said that with the advent of "conditional and restricted democracies," what might be called "the air of formal freedom" is producing some changes.

Ikeda: I see. For democracy to truly advance, incessant dialogue and action are required.

This calls to mind for me the thoughts of Nichiren, who stated that "a king sees his people as his parents"[2] and demanded that rulers "act as hands and feet for the multitude of people."[3] In other words, in true democracy, the people come foremost and the leaders are secondary, with the role of serving the people's needs.

But in reality, what do we see? The view that the nation takes priority and its people are secondary to it is still deep rooted. The leaders who should act as the hands and feet of the people instead look down on them and treat them as tools for their own ends. This is the source of the misery of the people.

A true democracy reverses this relationship and restores liberty and human rights to the people.

Power Acts to Suppress Popular Movements

Esquivel: Precisely.

The struggles of the peoples of Latin America have always been a contentious path characterized by the tension between the interests of those who hold power, both domestic and foreign, and the needs of those who are most unprotected.

In 2001, people's uprisings such as the protests involving beating pots and pans (*cacerolazos*) in Argentina and the "Tequila effect" in Mexico resulted in many casualties and the plundering of people's resources and savings—I refer in Argentina to the people's movement that brought about the downfall of the government of President Fernando de la Rúa.

Many other countries experienced similar situations, such as the severe economic crisis in Ecuador and the popular uprising against it, the grave situation in Paraguay, and also the conflicts, hunger, and desolation afflicting several Central American and Caribbean nations.

Numerous Latin American nations are facing various problems of this sort. What is clear is that the old power structures remain firmly in place, in spite of the passage of time. Violence arising from various ideological factions has also left its mark on the lives of the people.

I had the opportunity to attend a conference of survivors of concentration camps during the military dictatorship in Argentina. They were members of agricultural cooperatives that had been formed in the countryside from the 1960s to 1970s in Argentina to promote local growth and improve productivity, but they were destroyed by the military dictatorship. Many of their leaders were kidnapped and their whereabouts are still unknown. Similar situations occurred in Paraguay, Chile, and Brazil.

I believe that you, President Ikeda, have personally experienced similar incidents reflecting these extremely complicated circumstances.

Ikeda: Only to a small degree, but I did get a glimpse of the situation.

I made my second trip to Brazil in 1966. It was two years after the military coup, and many intellectual and cultural leaders were being persecuted and driven into exile. Wherever I went, I was under police surveillance. This was the result of false claims made about me to the authorities, mostly originating from certain Japanese who denounced me as a communist or an advocate of violence. The gymnasium where the final meeting of my visit was held was surrounded by two hundred police officers.

When I tried to visit Brazil again in 1974, my visa application was rejected, and I was forced to cancel my plans. The next time I was able to visit Brazil was in 1984.

In 1993, I visited Argentina, Chile, Paraguay, and made my fourth visit to Brazil. In comparison to the period of military rule, it seemed a completely different country. I sensed that peace had been restored and the tide of democracy was rising in the lives of the people.

Esquivel: I see that even you experienced some of the oppression of the period of military dictatorship, too.

In Brazil, 1966 was a very ominous period of the oppression of the military dictatorship, which you experienced personally. There was persecution and police surveillance, and anyone who attempted to offer words of hope to the oppressed was silenced.

I had similar experiences in Brazil in 1975 and 1980. I was arrested and imprisoned twice, though I was eventually released through the intervention of Cardinal Paulo Evaristo Arns of the Roman Catholic

Archdiocese of São Paulo and popular mobilization. As soon as I was freed, I was expelled from the country.

Ikeda: You have been arrested in and expelled from Paraguay, Chile, Uruguay, and Ecuador. Throughout it all, your indomitable convictions have continued to shine brilliantly and you have kept up your fight against indescribable hardships.

Your example reminds me of a passage from the poem "Martín Fierro" by the great poet of your homeland, José Hernández (1834–86):

To overcome dangers
and get out of the deepest pit,
I tell you this from experience:
more than swords or spears
you'll be helped by the confidence
that a man has in himself.[4]

Most of those in power care nothing for the sufferings of the people and are only concerned with preserving their special privileges. But their oppression of the people is actually a demonstration of their fear of the people. They fear and despise the possibility that the people may unite and stand up, wise and strong.

Esquivel: The brilliant epic poem "Martín Fierro" from which you have just quoted depicts the lives of the ordinary countrymen, the *paisanos,* forced to endure the vagaries of misfortune, subjected to oppression and injustice, driven from their homes by the authorities and experiencing crushing poverty.

José Hernández captures, with expressive justice and a rich poetic voice, the spirit of resistance and the powerful will of those who persevere in upholding their values and refusing to be vanquished. He describes those whose ordinary lives are suddenly disrupted by the shifts in power. The gauchos, cowboys of the South American pampas, were treated unjustly, conscripted and sent to the borders, and forced to fight against the indigenous peoples, who were also the victims of a campaign of plunder and expulsion known as "The Conquest of the Desert." The rulers made the soldiers fight the indigenous peoples, setting the poor against the poor and reaping the spoils of war for themselves.

Through his sufferings, Fierro, the gaucho who is the subject of the poem, learns to survive in the most extreme circumstances and stand up to injustice without compromising his beliefs. He experiences many troubles because of his ignorance of the laws created by the powerful, but he keeps pressing forward, finding new paths to remain unvanquished by the rulers who are trying to control him through their orders.

José Hernández was a perceptive observer of the life of the gauchos, penetrating the psychology of these emblematic figures of his times. Fierro's life continues to reflect the circumstances of our times. The troubles he encountered have far from come to an end but still persist in the lives of the poor and dispossessed, exploited by the powers who both then and now dominate our world. These billions of poor and hungry suffer from the same evil, the intolerance of the domination of the powerful that leaves no room for others.

Throughout history, the people have suffered the emergence of oppressive regimes. Though the forms may vary, they all operate by the same scheme. Yet the people still retain the power of resistance to overcome this oppression and survive. To make that possible, we need to forge alliances with many different kinds of groups and create new choices, free from the influence of the regimes, in society, government, the economy, and culture.

Ikeda: That is a very perceptive observation.

On a different level, our movement has also been persecuted and falsely denounced by forces that wish to suppress the power of the people. We have triumphed in spite of that cold reality. We have not let ourselves be stopped by the harsh tempests of adversity.

When I was arrested on false charges by the authorities, my mentor Josei Toda courageously declared: "Without a fight, justice will be defeated. The Soka Gakkai is in the right, so we cannot afford to lose; we must win at all costs. That's why it's so important that we fight. Lions are distinguished by their roar."

I will never forget those words.

Esquivel: I could not agree more. Without struggle, justice cannot prevail. For more than three decades I have observed the actions of the people of Latin America, shared their lives, and studied the path to liberation.

"What has brought us to this situation?" I have asked myself. "What could have been done to avoid it, what could the people have done to prevent it from reaching this point?"

But from my experience, I can say that the oppressed peoples will not remain silent forever. The time eventually comes when certain sectors of society react, abandon their passivity and their accepting attitudes toward government and the sectors of power, and reclaim their rights.

The people possess great diversity and cultural wealth. Men and women alike have immense natural and intellectual resources enabling every citizen to lead lives of dignity.

Ikeda: I agree completely. The people possess tremendous innate resources. It is a great tragedy of history when they remain unaware of their strength and allow themselves to be dominated.

I am reminded of an anecdote about an elephant that was chained to a stake as a calf. Even after it had grown large enough to pull out the stake and be free, it remained chained to the stake, because that was what it was used to.

If the people stand up with self-confidence, they are an enormous force. The crucial point is awakening the people to their worth and dignity so that they can demonstrate their true strength.

Urgent Actions or Long-term Structural Reform— Which Is the Priority?

Esquivel: That is indeed an issue worth pursuing.

With regard to Latin America, the people have become accustomed to structures and mechanisms of control that have prevented the advance to the construction of a new paradigm of life. Reality reveals the faces of millions of impoverished human beings who have been pitilessly subjected to social and institutional injustice.

For example, the issue of land ownership is one of Latin America's greatest tragedies. It is an urgent problem for the indigenous peoples and small farmers who have been driven off their lands. The authorities and government officials have worked hand in hand to create mass migrations of indigenous peoples and small farmers who have been expelled from their lands. These disenfranchised peoples have poured into areas on the outskirts of the major cities, creating slums whose residents are not even treated as human beings.

The confiscated lands are then handed over to large domestic and foreign enterprises that raze the forests that are the life support of local communities, destroying the balance of nature and causing the devastation of their habitats and cultures.

The great powers, focused on geopolitical, strategic, and military interests, vie for hegemony and world domination with no concern for its cost at the local level, in people's lives.

The problem is the same for both indigenous communities and small- and medium-scale farmers: the loss of their rights to land ownership, their identity and values, and the water and resource shortages created by large-scale agriculture.

What's needed is to reinforce networks of mutual support to protect the rights of the people.

Ikeda: You have firmly allied yourselves with the oppressed and see the world through their eyes.

We of the Soka Gakkai have always fought resolutely to aid the oppressed and suffering. In the past, the Soka Gakkai was ridiculed as an organization of the poor and sick, but I have always taken pride in that. We have succeeded in building a vast network of the people for peace and justice, altering the history of Japanese religion—which up until our time had always ingratiated itself to the authorities—and striving to transform society.

The arrogant established powers seek to divide the people. To oppose that, we must unite in the cause of justice and human rights. People's movements also need to be aware of the error of focusing solely on their own immediate situation. Only a movement based on an awareness of broader human rights and interests can bring fundamental changes to society.

Esquivel: That's what it's all about. In fact, there are times when the social movements in Latin America reveal their weakness. Though they may be successful in rallying the people, they fail to realize concrete political actions to effect the changes desired by the people.

For example, in many cases, they focus on situations requiring urgent attention and as a result lose sight of the important and necessary, overlooking the mid- and long-term planning needed to achieve the structural changes the people desire.

Urgent needs are given priority—such as feeding the needy, joining the indigenous peoples and small farmers in their struggles against the confiscation of their lands, and meeting the needs of those suffering from social marginalization and exclusion. While it is true that such activities need to be prioritized, most of the responses end up being palliative, without resolving the fundamental structural issues that are the causes of poverty and social exclusion.

At a recent meeting of SERPAJ, we addressed this issue of priorities and we agreed on the need to consider the two aspects of what is urgent and what is important. There are cases in which the urgent and the important are the same. There are also cases in which focus on the urgent leads to overlooking the important. In other words, while putting out the small fires we consider urgent, we overlook the important thing. A decision must be made each time which is the priority—putting out the small fire or building structures for safety and prevention so that fires don't break out in the first place.

Ikeda: What is the basis for that decision?

Esquivel: Again and again, one has to consider the basic purpose or fundamental goal of the activity in question. It is necessary to continually ask ourselves if we are taking the right path. In the event that we find ourselves going in the wrong direction, we must revise and correct our course, acquiring the capacity to reflect the basis of the fundamental purpose of each action and questioning whether the action we are taking is really a priority or not.

In Latin America, conflicts, problems, and economic and political interests are deeply intertwined, making structural changes absolutely necessary. The people's participation—along with the authorities, although that is not always possible—is required to achieve social and public policies that establish solidarity and build peaceful coexistence between people and communities.

Ikeda: The establishment of enduring bonds of solidarity among awakened people is crucial, as is education. This is the key to overcoming poverty and the structural problems that create it.

In addition, as you say, leadership is needed. Leaders of robust intelligence and character, capable individuals who can build such all-embracing, enduring solidarity among the people, are needed to deal with the urgent problems of life and livelihood while also steadily pursuing mid- and long-term structural reform for society.

The Triumphant Sun of the People's Victory

Ikeda: Argentina has an impressive history of the victory of the people. The transfer from military dictatorship to civilian rule achieved by you and other champions of human rights is part of that history.

Looking farther back, there was the May Revolution. In May 1810, the people of Argentina forced the Viceroy of the Viceroyalty of the Río de la Plata, Baltasar Hidalgo de Cisneros y de la Torre (1756–1829), to step down and established a new and independent government. The bicentennial of that event occurred in 2010.

The leaders of the May Revolution fought for human rights, equality, freedom of the press and thought, the end of slavery, public education, and other noble ideals that rallied the people to their cause and inspired them to rise up.

Negotiations between the revolution's representatives and the Viceroy, who was determined to remain in the seat of power, continued for some time. Eventually, the people surrounded the building where the discussions were taking place and angrily demanded an end to the Viceroy's oppressive rule. The cry for revolution arising from the hearts of the people was unstoppable, and eventually the Viceroy was forced to resign. This nonviolent, bloodless revolution was a brilliant achievement.

I understand that in Argentina today May remains the starting point for independence and liberty and the month is regarded as symbolic of the victory of the people. The sun in the center of your national flag is known as the Sun of May, referring to the sun that arose on that day of independence. To me it seems to represent the sun of revolution illuminating the people and dispelling the darkness of oppression with the light of liberty and independence.

Esquivel: It is true that since then, or even before that, until the present time, the Argentine people have adopted various responses to oppressive situations.

Some groups have held that the only response to the ruling elite is violent opposition from those below in the form of armed revolution. I have seen this throughout the Latin American continent, where movements and groups of guerrillas have emerged in different countries for decades.

Other groups have attempted to resolve the problem within the confines of the law and society's institutions. These groups are varied in character, some arising from churches or established nongovernmental organizations, while others are ideologically based or have other philosophical foundations. Still others are groups formed to seek the amelioration of a particular problem or issue. And there are also other movements with the same bases as those I have already described that arise to advocate for the victims of the violence against the lack of response from the institutions of the state.

The actions of these groups may appear weak, but they influence other citizens and engender policies and institutions that achieve the recovery of justice and human rights. The activities of human rights groups create a climate in which the people stop being spectators and take on the role of protagonists, generating new forms of popular participation.

Ikeda: A new age is initiated when the people take leadership. The initiative of the people, no longer satisfied to remain bystanders, must be tapped and harnessed.

The violent opposition advocated by certain factions is not the wish of the majority of the people. The sole and fundamental solution is nonviolent, gradual change. And the foundation of nonviolence is the spiritual force of courage.

Esquivel: Indeed. Nonviolence is the foundation for the activities of all these groups.

In most cases they intuitively choose nonviolence, without fully grasping its scope. Generally, the reaction of the people to oppression is instinctive and spontaneous. It is not the result of conscious reasoning, but over time and through their actions, their goals become increasingly concrete and the significance of their movement becomes clear. Some examples are movements for human rights, labor conflicts, and demands for recognition by certain sectors of society.

But in all learning you have to start with the first step. An ancient Chinese sage—I believe it was Lao Tzu—said: "The tree which needs two arms to span its girth sprang from the tiniest shoot . . . A journey of a thousand miles began with a single step."[5]

Ikeda: I am happy to learn that you are aware of these concepts of Asian thought.

Your experience as a man of action and actual struggle for human rights imbues your words with especial significance. Learning through action is critical. Growth is achieved through struggle.

When Gandhi was incarcerated for his participation in the nonviolent movement, he used his time in prison to read. One of the books he read was *Faust* by Goethe (1749–1832), in which we find the statement, "In the beginning was the Deed."[6]

Goethe also wrote in *Faust*: "He only earns both freedom and existence / Who must reconquer them each day."[7] Goethe's perceptive insight was that only through action, through struggle, can we enjoy freedom.

The Need for Organizations to Fortify Human Solidarity

Esquivel: Action is always crucial. We learn by doing. After taking the first step, we must continue building day by day. We need to engage in the continuing struggle to build what I call "spaces of freedom," in resistance, consciousness, and action.

At that initial stage, we faced behaviors that we had to overcome as both individuals and collectives.

First, we had to learn to transcend individualism: to realize that together it is possible to achieve our goals, but alone we cannot.

Second, the need for reflection and action—that is to say, to abandon the immobility from which nothing positive can emerge.

Third, we needed to learn to make effective use of the mass media. Although the national media might be subject to censorship, there are always other alternatives available or that we can create ourselves, including opening channels of communication in the international media.

Fourth, we had to overcome fear. Oppressors employ institutionalized violence to obstruct social activism and paralyze any opposition from the people to their interests. For example, the military promoted hatred and suspicion at the individual and collective level, employing it as a form of psychological warfare.

They repeated such messages as "Shun them," "They are enemies of the homeland," "We are here to guarantee your peace and security," "Do not allow your children to get involved with subversive human rights groups," "They are communists and subversives," and so forth.

These kinds of messages are aimed at generating suspicion and fear.

Ikeda: This was precisely the situation in prewar Japan.

The standard ploy of the authorities when attacking and persecuting an individual or a group is to unjustly label them in a way that rouses people's suspicions. We must never forget that this sort of thing can occur in every age.

Esquivel: And in all cases, in addition to their lies, the oppressors try to establish a permanent state of fear in people's hearts.

How can the fears and immobility that oppressors strive to implant in people's minds be overcome? The answer is that each person must shake off their inner chains and discard their preconceived notions, so that they can begin to see reality in another way and realize that only if they unite and succeed in organizing themselves can they break free from the state of oppression in which they live.

Ikeda: From my own experience, I agree with you completely. Unity is the only way for the people to triumph over oppression, and organizations are needed to act as pillars promoting the solidarity of the people.

This has been amply demonstrated by the great popular movement of the twentieth century led by the likes of Gandhi and Martin Luther King, Jr. (1926–68). One of the lessons of the twentieth century, with its two world wars and incessant violence, is that organizations working together for peace are an absolute necessity. Individualism may seem a form of freedom, but in the end individuals can be easily defeated. Solidarity and teamwork are crucial.

Buddhism strives to promote humanism, respect for life, peace, culture, and education. It teaches the need to overcome differences of race, religion, and culture and form bonds of friendship, to freely join together in solidarity. This is the aim of our movement.

Esquivel: I have the most profound respect for your efforts in building the Soka Gakkai as a magnificent organization for peace, culture, and education.

Ikeda: I am deeply honored by your words, which are a tremendous source of encouragement to all our members. As you noted earlier, we must create new paradigms of life that promote the practice of nonviolence.

Buddhism clearly articulates the keys to promoting unity through nonviolence in its teaching of the four methods employed by bodhisattvas to attract others to Buddhism.

The first is giving, not only material goods but also encouragement and a philosophy of life that dispels anxiety and fear.

The second is kindly speech, or dialogue based on consideration for others.

The third is actions that benefit others.

The fourth is cooperation, working together with others to do good deeds.

These four kinds of conduct provide the guiding principles for a nonviolent people's movement.

As I noted earlier, our founding president, Tsunesaburo Makiguchi, opposed Japan's militaristic government during the war and died in prison as a result. Our second president, Josei Toda, was imprisoned with Makiguchi but lived to be released and carry on the mandate of his mentor. Toda was utterly opposed to war and determined to rally the people and build an unshakable organization for peace.

The movement carried out by the Soka Gakkai is based on the Nichiren Buddhist philosophy of the sanctity of life and, inheriting the spirit of Makiguchi and Toda, aims to create world peace. That is why I have actively sought out individuals of differing ideologies and beliefs to engage in dialogue.

We need to overcome our differences and work together for the peace of humanity. That is the spirit of dialogue advocated by the Nichiren Buddhist teaching of "establishing the correct teaching for the peace of the land." In accord with that teaching, I have met and established channels of communication with many leading thinkers in Japan and around the world.

As I have said repeatedly, I regard this exchange with you and the friendship we have formed as my greatest honors.

Esquivel: Thank you. I would also like to reiterate my gratitude to you for this wonderful opportunity to engage in dialogue.

How to Avoid Repeating Tragedy

Esquivel: There is another issue that I would like to discuss at this point—the immunity that most Latin American countries, in spite of their shift to democracy, have given to the perpetrators of violence under military dictatorships.

In Argentina we have begun to put these individuals on trial. It took twenty years of legal struggles, but we have finally nullified the Full Stop Law and the Law of Due Obedience that protected them. We succeeded in accomplishing this through the persistent action of human rights organizations, the courage of women and men committed to the pursuit of truth and justice, who called for no immunity and trial and punishment of those responsible.

Ikeda: Yes, the Argentine people have displayed an unflinching spirit of truth and justice in their battle for human rights.

In order to prevent the same thing from happening again, it is critical to set history straight and learn from it. No matter how painful it may be, a new future cannot be opened without a correct view of the past.

Esquivel: Definitely. As far as I am concerned, I do not agree with those who claim to have forgotten what occurred or who say that we should not think about the past but concern ourselves solely with the future.

It is important to emphasize that the defense of human rights goes beyond the ideological positions of right and left; it is a matter of human dignity. Only subjugated and dominated peoples, motivated by fear or calculated amnesia, refuse to look at their pasts and tolerate or conceal injustices with impunity.

Ikeda: It is important to make justice and truth absolutely clear to all.

The British historian Arnold J. Toynbee (1889–1975), with whom I engaged in a dialogue, summed up the lesson to be learned from the struggle against the Nazis as follows: "Civilization cannot ever be taken for granted. Its price is eternal vigilance and ceaseless spiritual effort."[8] Toynbee actually met and spoke with the Nazi leader Adolf Hitler (1889–1945).

Speaking of his wartime job reporting on international affairs, Toynbee told me that he strongly felt at the time that if he were to be unemotional and detached in his treatment of the Holocaust, as if he were giving a weather report, he would in fact not be able to present an accurate record of the situation, because ignoring the moral implications of the atrocity would have been a kind of silent acquiescence to it.

In other words, one cannot be neutral in the face of evil. Failing to fight against evil is collusion with evil.

Esquivel: Precisely because that is so, we still face an arduous struggle in relation to our past.

During the military dictatorship in Argentina, the Navy was one of the armed forces that acted with the greatest cruelty. The clandestine detention center of the Escuela Superior de Mecánica de la Armada (the Higher School of Mechanics of the Navy), where the Museo de la Memoria (Museum of Memory) now operates, epitomized this.

Today we are progressing step by step, and for this we have established a dialogue with the Armed Forces. As chair of the Faculty of Social Sciences at the University of Buenos Aires, together with those enrolled in my course on the culture of peace and human rights, I am focusing on dialogues with the Navy.

The current officers and members of the naval force did not take part in the events during the military dictatorship, but many of them feel they bear institutional responsibility for the terror exercised by the armed forces at that time.

It is important to define the role of the military in a democracy. We are engaged in a dialogue with the military to ensure that the curriculum of military training stresses military service as a form of service as an individual citizen to the people of the nation. This program is coordinated jointly with the Inter-American Institute of Human Rights (IIHR), belonging to the Organization of American States (OAS). Another of the educational initiatives being undertaken is with the Federal Police.

We are also working on a joint project with the Anne Frank House of the Netherlands and the police of that nation for the training of the new members of the police force.

These advances are part of building democracy, fostering a shared awareness among citizens and the police force of being fellow members of society rather than antagonists, engendering mutual understanding, and promoting social responsibility and engagement.

Ikeda: I have heard that a naval officer has also testified to some of the barbaric acts the Navy carried out during the military dictatorship in Argentina.

Esquivel: According to the testimony of Naval Captain Adolfo Scilingo, between 1977 and 1979 he threw thirty prisoners, alive and naked, into the sea from a plane.

The National Criminal and Administrative Court (Audiencia Nacional) in Madrid sentenced him to 640 years in prison (in April 2005), and he is currently serving his sentence in Spain.

While still in Argentina, Captain Scilingo visited me with his wife and two attorneys, and we talked for two hours. He appeared to be an anguished person with a strong conscience.

However, he said that he did everything he did, including throwing thirty prisoners into the sea on two "death flights," because he believed he was fighting a war to save the country from the clutches of international communism.

He asked me if I thought it was right that he should go to Spain to stand trial when his superiors refused to assume any responsibility. I told him that this decision must be a matter of his personal conscience, if he wished to make amends to some extent for his actions.

He decided to go to Spain and stand trial, and as a result of his testimony, he was punished and expelled from the navy. I testified as a witness in the Madrid trial, where I recounted to the court the discussion that Captain Scilingo and I had before he made his decision.

Totalitarianism Emerges from Spiritual Vacuum

Ikeda: That is most valuable testimony on your part.

In your speech at the Nobel Laureates Forum in Nagoya, Japan, 1988, you argued that humanity had succumbed to materialism and was dominated by the craving for power. That state of "spiritual hunger," you said, was one of the factors that could trigger genocide. That is why, you stressed, we must remember the horror of the two world wars of the past, and in particular the tragedies of Hiroshima and Nagasaki, and awaken the consciences of people the world over.[9]

Esquivel: Yes, that's what I believe. Unfortunately, in several countries in Europe, the United States, and Latin America, there seem to be certain sectors of the population that yearn for the return of fascism, Nazism, and totalitarian regimes—particularly young people who have no historical memory or critical awareness.

This phenomenon has to do with the failure of our educational systems, lack of historical memory, and the shallow exaltation of authoritarian systems by the media. As an educator, I can also perceive signs of hope, of social and cultural resistance in the young men and women in our universities, schools, and social organizations. However, at the same time I see great risks and concerns, particularly a tendency to become absorbed by materialism and consumer society, as if this were the path to happiness and the ultimate goal of the human being.

The risk I perceive is the loss of spirituality—preserving ritual and custom but without any depth of consciousness and spirit.

Ikeda: I, too, fear that we may succumb to the same condition, and I agree with your analysis of the present state of affairs. Material civilization advanced at an unprecedented pace during the twentieth century and unarguably made our lives easier, but we cannot deny the fact that our spiritual progress has been overlooked.

Rather, excessive dependence on materialism leads to the erosion of the spiritual and robs us of the will to realize our full humanity.

The Italian philosopher Norberto Bobbio (1909–2004) fought in the resistance movement against Italian fascism, and was imprisoned twice. In response to the question of what must be done to prevent the emergence of future dictators, he said that democracy needs individuals who can think critically and independently. It was not individuals who were roused by the speeches of Benito Mussolini (1883–1945), but a mob, he said.[10]

This is a truth we must never forget. I believe that fostering individuals who can think for themselves is the supreme way to fortify democracy.

One of the Buddhist scriptures, the *Dhammapada,* states: "The self indeed is the lord of self; who else indeed could be lord? By the self indeed, when well tamed, one obtains a lord who is hard to obtain."[11] Another scripture, the *Udānavarga,* states: "The sage attains clear wisdom through self-control."[12]

The "self" here is not the small self dominated by selfishness or greed but rather the self characterized by discipline and the drive for perfection, filled with compassion, love for humanity, wisdom, courage, and a robust will. It is a self that has vanquished egotism, is thoughtful, possesses a rational, critical mind, and, motivated by compassion and love, seeks to cooperate with others. The formation of such a self is the core for cooperation among the people.

Esquivel: From these words of the Buddhist scriptures, I can see that Buddhism articulates a process of deep spiritual work for the individual.

Religions are also facing a great challenge—the challenge of forging relationships with each other and sharing the gifts of the spirit with other creeds, without losing their specific identities.

Ikeda: That is what makes dialogues among religions so important.

It is the role of a world religion to restore the spirituality and enhance the moral fiber of a society that has lost its spiritual and moral compasses and is driven solely by materialism.

In Buddhism, for example, the basic moral principles are as follows.

First, not to kill. This is the spirit of nonviolence and compassion. This principle forbids allowing anger to cause war or conflict, harming and killing others.

The second Buddhist moral principle is not to steal. This forbids the greed that motivates us to take the belongings of others, and can be said to also apply to appropriating and exploiting the resources of others.

The third is not to engage in sexual misconduct. This moral principle aims at controlling the base impulses inherent in life by establishing an ethic of responsibility, mutual respect, and equality in male–female relationships. In contemporary terms, this can be regarded as applying not only to gender but also equality and mutual respect among races, cultures, ethnic groups, and professions.

The fourth principle is not to lie. It forbids deceiving people through our words. Manipulating others through language for profit or to destroy the natural environment is outlawed by this principle.

The moral principles of Buddhism are all based on equal respect for all life.

Life, Not Material Goods, Is the Essential Value

Esquivel: This ethical deterioration and loss of spirituality that we have mentioned are not limited to a country or a region. Today national sovereignties are also being lost, and the world has become a large global market, where merchandise is worth more than the life of the people.

Africa, Latin America, and Asia are continents possessing great resources for the lives and development of their peoples, but the mechanisms of exploitation to which they are subjected persist and have led people to hunger, misery, and marginality.

I recently received a very disturbing message by e-mail: the image of an African child about to starve to death, and a vulture waiting for the child to die. Another image shows a mother who cannot feed her child holding him in her arms while he dies. I have personally witnessed scenes like this on the Latin American continent, in rural areas, in indigenous settlements, in slums and shantytowns. This is the reality of the injustice and despoliation so many people are facing.

The companies behind this exploitation have no feelings or pity; their only interest is the resources of countries they call the "Third World." They are not interested in the human cost of the predation to which they are subjecting so many people.

We have a long way to go to awaken their consciences and arouse their will to do good.

Ikeda: That is an important warning. It is said that today more than a billion people live on less than a dollar a day.[13]

The rise in grain prices (since autumn 2006) is leading to the danger of food shortages in various countries. It is predicted that this will subject an additional 40 million people to hunger and that the number suffering nutritional deficiencies will rise to 963 million.

Since 1974, I have been proposing the establishment of a world food bank, to prevent food, the foundation of human life, from becoming the pawn of wars and unchecked market forces. We need to restructure our world from the perspective of life instead of money.

Esquivel: In addition to the problem of hunger, today war and armed conflict have created millions of refugees. Their numbers are frightening. In Colombia alone, there are more than two million internally displaced people who have lost everything and live in extreme situations.

In the region of the African Great Lakes, ethnic wars and those waged by huge economic interests—such as the exploitation of diamonds, gold, and minerals—have caused more than three million deaths, while thousands of people die of malnutrition, hunger, or as victims of violence at the hands of murderous groups and the armed forces. The survivors are lost in the jungle and displaced in their own homeland.

In an increasingly interdependent world, people are affected by events that take place thousands of miles away, in different countries and cultures. Likewise, we live in an age in which changes in international relations are occurring at an ever-accelerating pace, and we are all subjected to a dynamic of sudden transformations.

The former bipolar world ended with the disintegration of the Soviet Union, which has been followed by bloody conflicts in the Balkan Peninsula and numerous other places. The end of the Cold War was an important change, but not a fair one. When the United States became the sole hegemonic power, the world became unipolar. This development had a strong impact on relations between the countries of the South and the countries of the North. The countries of the South are increasingly looking for ways to distance themselves from the center of power.

The Dream and Challenges of a United Latin America

Ikeda: When considering the direction in which our world should advance, I see efforts at regional integration as offering a solution to conflict and poverty.

In his dialogue with me, President Aylwin of Chile said that the dream of the founders of the countries of South America was a unified Latin America.[14] This vision of a vast unified continent is sometimes called the Bolivarian dream.

At present the economic federation Mercosur (Southern Common Market) is evolving in Latin America. Its members include Argentina, Brazil, Paraguay, Uruguay, and Venezuela, representing about 250 million people and a combined GDP of 1,000 billion US dollars (as of 2006). Chile, Bolivia, Peru, Ecuador, and Columbia are all associate countries, and hopes are rising for the emergence of a stable common market on the continent.

Conquering poverty is strongly linked to eliminating the factors that contribute to social unrest and crime. And if economic ties also contribute to promoting culture and peace awareness, the prospects for regional integration become even brighter.

Esquivel: A united Latin America was the dream of our ancestors, who fought for the liberation of our peoples, and it remains the dream of many who are still working at present to make it come true.

You have expressed your hopes for Mercosur. We believe it is a valid initiative, which should be strengthened but also expanded.

Originally Mercosur sought to benefit the large industrial corporations, leaving behind the needs of small and medium-sized rural and industrial producers. This has deepened strong economic asymmetries and inequalities, making it necessary to rethink the policies and orientation of Mercosur to ameliorate this situation.

The Latin American common market needs to go beyond economic agreements to strengthen cultural and political ties, expanding integration with other countries in the region interested in joining. It is also necessary to create more just and equitable relations between the members, in particular with the smaller countries.

Ikeda: That is an important point. Some thinkers point to the birth of the EU in Europe as leading the way to a multipolar world as it promotes the creation of a Union of South American Nations, an African Union, and an East Asian Community.

At present, we may be seeing a tug of war between the centripetal force leading to global homogenization and the centrifugal force of multipolarization. The problem arises because while the spread of information is leading toward increasing global homogenization, efforts at fortifying and reinforcing the solidarity of humankind are not keeping pace, and the necessary responses to ameliorate the negative effects of global homogenization are not taking place.

Gandhi's wish was "to wipe every tear from every eye."[15] My mentor Josei Toda declared his desire to eliminate misery from the Earth.

Such awareness of the sanctity of life, empathy for the suffering of other human beings, and the desire to alleviate their pain must transcend regions, national borders, and all obstacles. As long as there are those whose human rights are threatened, we cannot rest. Spreading that spirit and behavior is the way to transform the underlying dynamic of the age.

Buddhism teaches that the basic reason for the Buddha's appearance in the world lies in his behavior as a human being—behavior symbolized in the Lotus Sutra by Bodhisattva Never Disparaging.

As his name indicates, Bodhisattva Never Disparaging afforded everyone the highest respect and veneration. Though they might attack and abuse him, he would press his palms together in a gesture of reverence and declare, "I would never dare disparage you, because you are all certain to attain buddhahood!"[16] By this means, he awakened people to the sacred life within each of them.

Disrespecting the life of another is evil. Unfortunately, it is a trait evidenced by many in power. The wicked path of disrespecting life not only corrupts the individual who follows it but also weakens and destroys nations and societies.

The people need to become strong and wise to carefully oversee those in positions of authority. I think it could be said that this has been the aim of all your struggles up to now, Dr. Esquivel.

Esquivel: I am very grateful for your evaluation of my efforts in those terms.

With respect to dignity and engagement with others, the peoples of Latin America have had numerous experiences. In their shared resistance to oppression, they have learned valuable lessons about life and living together, about establishing interwoven human relationships based on common values and needs.

The same could be said of Japan. Your country has managed over time to overcome the trauma of war and the distressing results—the spiritual wounds—arising from it, such as foreign occupation. The Japanese people had the capacity and the work ethic to rebuild their country and achieve social and political stability.

These achievements were due to their ability to integrate the technological and scientific advances of the Western world while preserving their unique culture and values fostered over millennia. By assimilating the forms of development of a foreign culture, the

West, without losing their identity, they were able to discover ways to carry out structural changes and achieve their objectives in an orderly way.

From Latin America, Japan is generally seen as a developed country with great economic potential that has retained its ancestral cultural paradigms and values. At the same time, Japan is also seen as a nation that, while adopting the positive characteristics of foreign Western culture, has also been absorbed by the vortex of the capitalist and consumerist system.

Learning from the Cultural Legacies of Others

Ikeda: That is a perceptive insight. Throughout history Japan has developed its own distinct culture while absorbing much from other cultures.

After World War II, Japan actively adopted the American lifestyle and attained astonishing economic growth. In that process, Japan swung like a pendulum between its traditional culture and the foreign culture.

Today many raise the alarm that Japan is being overwhelmed by global supercapitalism and in danger of losing its fundamental identity.

Esquivel: When incorporating values from other cultures, it is crucial to both preserve one's own cultural memory and to separate the wheat from the chaff—to select the beneficial elements of the other culture and synthesize them with one's own cultural values.

Ikeda: That is an important problem. All of the peoples on our planet possess unique traditional cultures fostered throughout their long histories.

When the Spanish arrived in pre-Columbian America, as is well known, they encountered many different peoples, each possessing their distinctive culture. Mayan civilization, Aztec civilization, and Inca civilization, for example—which extended to the southern

Andes in modern northern Argentina—were all flourishing as highly developed cultures distinct from European civilization.

Esquivel: As you have noted, the indigenous peoples of Latin America had achieved great technological and scientific advances. They had developed the science of astronomy to a remarkable degree of precision. They employed this science and technology in feats of hydraulic engineering applied to daily life, developing techniques unknown in those times in Europe.

The richness and diversity of pre-Columbian culture and art—for example, architecture—are astounding in their expression and character, reminiscent of the great edifices like ziggurats or terraced-step pyramids of the Assyrian, Babylonian, and Egyptian cultures.

Their monumental sculpture, of great expressive richness, reveals their vision of the cosmos and their magnanimous spirituality. Only recently, after many centuries, has the worth of these civilizations been recognized and serious research on them commenced.

Ikeda: As you have noted, Incan architecture is renowned for its highly developed stone building techniques.

Professor Toynbee visited Machu Picchu and other Incan sites and praised them for their imposing strength: "As for the dressed masonry of the palaces, it is proof against the earthquakes that have made havoc of the baroque superstructures that the Spanish conquerors piled upon it. The Inca's reign may have been brief, but they built for eternity."[17]

The forms of stone architecture found throughout the Incan empire, which extended five thousand kilometers along the Andes from north to south, displayed remarkable uniformity, while also having diversity. It is said that it was built to harmonize with the varied topography of the Andes, with a conscious eye to harmony with nature and the scenery of each locale.

In addition, the Incas built forty thousand kilometers of roads and created beautiful terraced agricultural plots that enabled them to farm level fields on the steepest mountains. They also designed sophisticated irrigation systems that allowed them to cultivate large acreages. They exhibited an astonishing ingenuity and skill in transforming a harsh natural environment into one that could produce rich harvests.

The potato, which originated in the Andes, spread around the world, including Japan, and has been a staple food preventing hunger. We in Japan have also received this great boon from the peoples of the Andes.

Esquivel: The cultures that originated in Latin America, as the memory of our own ancestors tells us, were characterized by integration with the cosmos and by respect for Mother Earth.

Our ancestors a millennium ago sought in each other and in others, both in the village and in the world, a balance with divinity and the universe. When this balance was destroyed, the violence that we suffer today was generated.

Cartesian thinking has led to a fragmentation of ideas about the human being; it is necessary to return to a holistic view that regards the individual in union with Mother Nature and with the cosmos.

Ancient Peoples Were True Ecologists

Ikeda: The peoples of ancient Latin America respected the natural world, which provided them with many riches, as an expression of the divine. The ecological nature of Latin American culture—the belief that we humans are not the center of the world, but should exist in harmony with it—has pioneering significance even today.

The Min-On Concert Association (Min-On), which I founded, has invited numerous dance and other performing groups from Argentina and other Latin American nations to Japan, where they have presented the traditional culture of their homelands to Japanese audiences, including performances of Andean music and traditional dances of the indigenous peoples depicting their relations with nature and scenes of farming, herding, and fishing.

These dances and music, giving lively expression to the spirit of the people living in harmony with nature, have delighted Japanese audiences.

The Japanese people are fascinated and charmed by the Andes. Once when flying from Paraguay to Chile, I took a photograph of the majestic Andes, the cradle of such diversified culture. I treasure it to this day.

Esquivel: Your photographs have been presented in the exhibition "Dialogue with Nature," which has been seen in Argentina and other countries in Latin America.

The word "primitive" is usually used contemptuously, but the so-called "primitive peoples" are actually much more civilized than we are in their dialogue with nature. We are just now becoming aware of respect for Mother Earth, and we call it "being an ecologist."

But the ancestral peoples were always "ecologists." As far as listening to nature, apprehending its subtleties, and treasuring it, they deserved to be called "cultured," while we are ignoramuses.

Ikeda: Yes, I agree.

Though the grand scale of the natural world of Latin America is quite different from that of Japan, ancient Japanese culture also valued living in harmony with nature, appreciating the changes of the four seasons, and regarding nature as a friend.

With regard to the harmonious coexistence of humankind and nature, a superior wisdom illuminates the traditional cultures of Japan, other parts of Asia, and Latin America. We need to reawaken to that cultural wisdom, adopt it, and put it to use in all its aspects.

Culture is the flower of dialogue between human beings, and between humans and their natural setting and the universe as a whole. In addition, each culture grows and develops by encountering and absorbing new elements from other cultures.

Some say that the ancient mythology, philosophy, religion, poetry, literature, art, and the distinctive science and technology of every people remain alive in the depths of their beings. This "cultural memory" existing in multiple layers within the spirit of a people engenders their distinct value system, lifestyle, and moral code.

At this time in history, when a civilization based on the supremacy of materialism and blind devotion to the market economy is in the process of dominating the entire world, the cultures born from the unique experiences of each people have never had a more important role to play in the formation of a new culture of peace.

In Japan, too, we are seeing a reevaluation of Japan's unique culture, which is one of the forms of East Asian civilization, along with the cultures of China and Korea.

Esquivel: I agree that the issues of identity and cultural diversity are of paramount importance in this analysis. Today, in Latin America, there is also an urgent need to respect the diversity and cultural and spiritual identities of indigenous peoples, and there is an increasing desire to transmit the legacy of these cultures to future generations.

For example, one of the resoundingly successful social institutions in our indigenous cultures is the Council of Elders. It has been proposed that the administrators and faculty of schools, as well as the community in general, consult these councils and call upon the elders to transmit their knowledge and wisdom and the history of their peoples to new generations. Through this process of affirming and reestablishing the people's cultural identity and group membership, the mechanisms of acculturation to the dominant culture to which they are being subjected can be overcome.

Ikeda: In Buddhism, the experiences that have accumulated in the depths of a person's being over time are called karma.

Karma includes the memories created by our past experiences, as well as our identity, mind, intellect, emotions, and motivations. In that sense, karma is a latent energy that includes our memories. It exists not only within the individual but also in the depths of the spirit of a people, as well as in the deepest layers of the mind of the entire human race.

Cultural reestablishment is the creation of a new culture. Taking one's own culture as the core, we creatively transform our inner karma through encounters with others.

Esquivel: In fact, I mean the same thing when I say that we must preserve the memory of each people.

I also call it "shared memory." When peoples learn from each other's experiences, they enrich their own experiences and are able to seek the correct path to coexistence. These paths are sought in lifelong learning, conserving shared memory.

Japan and Argentina: Neighbors on Opposite Sides of the Globe

Ikeda: I agree completely.

Japan has a close relationship with Argentina and owes it a great debt of gratitude.

The year 2008 marked the centennial of official immigration from Japan to Argentina. There are 23,000 people of Japanese descent living in Argentina, and in that sense, Argentina has been very kind to Japan.[18]

The great master of the Argentine tango Astor Piazzolla (1921–92) reflected: "Getting to know people and sharing the spirit of self-development is a wonderful thing."[19] As Piazzolla demonstrated through music, interaction between people of different ethnic groups, countries, and cultures leads to new growth and self-development.

Min-On has introduced the wonderful Argentine tango to a wide spectrum of Japanese audiences, sponsoring annual performances since 1970—a total of forty times to date (as of 2009).

Listening to the tango, shining with the light of humanism, I am always reminded of my visit to Buenos Aires (February 1993) and my dear friend, the supreme master of the tango Osvaldo Pugliese (1905–95). Mr. Pugliese called the tango the folk music of the Argentine people, born from the hearts of the people. He said it had a human voice, which is why it always remained in tune with the people's feelings. I will never forget him declaring that his greatest teacher had always been the people.[20]

Japan and Argentina are neighbors on opposite sides of the globe. The heart-to-heart exchanges of peoples are the true mark of being a neighbor. Cultural exchange that, as Pugliese said, always remains in tune with the people's feelings, is absolutely indispensable.

Esquivel: It is very meaningful to reflect on the warm friendship and unity existing between Argentina and Japan.

Over a century has passed since the signing of the Treaty of Amity, Commerce and Navigation between our nations in 1898, and our relationship has grown stronger over time.

Argentina has received millions of immigrants from a wide variety of countries who have successfully integrated into the life of our people. Among them, Japanese immigrants have contributed greatly in the past and in the present to the development of the country.

The strengthening of cultural cooperation and good commercial relations between our two peoples has reinforced this unity. The establishment of Soka Gakkai International of Argentina has made a significant contribution to fortifying the friendly ties between our countries.

Many people here remember the series of commemorative events sponsored in Argentina and Japan by Min-On, which you founded, President Ikeda. The participation of Argentine artists such as José Marcelli and the great Osvaldo Pugliese, who have given so much to the popular music of Argentina, has contributed to world peace and unity.

Music is a language that reaches the heart and refreshes our lives.

Ikeda: Music and art know no borders.

Toson Shimazaki (1872–1943), a Japanese author whom I read in my youth, gave a lecture in Buenos Aires in 1936. During the lecture, Shimazaki displayed a copy of a masterpiece by the Japanese painter Sesshu (1420–1506) and spoke on the meaning of culture. He said:

> I believe that the most typical attributes of Argentina and Japan are the same. By most typical attribute, I mean affording supreme value to truly pure things. For example, even though the essence of things may be expressed in different ways because of differing specific features of Eastern and Western thinking, there will be no difference, in my opinion, in affording pure things the highest value. This is a firm and unshakable conviction in my soul.[21]

Superior culture blossoming from the fertile earth of life is the common treasure of all humankind. In 1990, the Tokyo Fuji Art Museum, which I founded, presented its exhibition "Eternal Treasures of Japanese Culture: Beauty and Spirit of Japan" at the Buenos Aires National Museum of Fine Arts, where it received an enthusiastic response.

One of the underlying currents that engendered the highest achievements of Japanese arts and culture is Buddhism, and the supreme Buddhist scripture, the Lotus Sutra. This can also be said of the great Chinese artistic treasure house, Dunhuang.[22]

That is why I believe that engaging in cultural exchange with other nations, while correctly introducing the Buddhist philosophy of life as manifested in its views of the universe, nature, birth and death, and nonviolence, is also an important contribution to peace. At the same time, sharing Buddhism is a gesture of appreciation to the peoples of China, the Korean Peninsula, and the rest of Asia, who transmitted Buddhism to Japan.

Japan must never falter in taking action to promote the peace and prosperity of the countries of Asia that it invaded during World

War II. In addition, as the only nation that has been subjected to atomic bombings, it is the mission, right, and duty of Japan to transmit the memories of Hiroshima and Nagasaki to the world and future generations.

It is my sincerest wish that Japan will win the increasing trust of the world's nations as a land of culture and peace.

Esquivel: I agree that conveying to the world and to the generations to come the culture, experience, and course taken by the Japanese people contributes greatly to world peace.

I know that, based on Japan's experience as the only nation that has fallen victim to atomic bombs, the SGI has organized exhibitions to raise public awareness of the threat of nuclear weapons that have been held in different parts of Argentina.

Ikeda: I am deeply appreciative of the sincere messages of congratulation that you sent us on each such occasion.

I would like to discuss the issue of the eradication of nuclear weapons on another occasion, but as you indicate, we have presented our exhibition at numerous venues in Argentina, including the University of Buenos Aires (Buenos Aires), the National University of Comahue (Neuquén), the National University of the Northeast (Resistencia), the Teatro Argentino de La Plata (La Plata), and the Teatro Auditorium in Mar del Plata. I am deeply grateful for the assistance we received from the staff at each venue.

Nothing would bring me greater joy than to see the youth and students of the next generation working in solidarity for the elimination of nuclear armaments. Youth are the main protagonists of the next generation.

Soka University in Tokyo is also conducting academic and educational exchanges with 106 universities in forty-four other nations and territories including your country (as of May 2009). International students are the great treasure of the world. As the founder of Soka University, I am always striving to ensure that the days that our students from various countries spend studying in Japan will be productive and nurturing, and that they will grow into leaders of outstanding ability.

I also pray for and watch over our Soka University students who are studying in Argentina and other countries and territories, hoping they will make the most of this valuable experience and grow into capable individuals contributing positively to global peace and prosperity.

Esquivel: For us, it is a joy to know that there are students from Soka University studying in Buenos Aires, eager to participate in the challenge of learning and sharing their experiences with other young people.

This exchange of experiences is always enriching and encourages young people to become aware of the reality and life of other peoples. It allows them to verify that, despite all the challenges, there is always the light and hope of building a better world for all.

Ikeda: Indeed, youth are as you say the light of hope for building a better world.

In 1996, a class of fourth-grade elementary school students in your country sent me a message.

It contained twenty questions, including: "Did you lose a loved one in a war?" "How did you feel when Japan went to war?" "At what age did you start to fight for world peace? What problems did you face?" and "I understand that to avoid violence we need to engage in sincere dialogue and make an effort to see our friends' good points. What else is important?"

I was delighted at this expression of an earnest wish for peace from these children, emissaries from the future, and I responded to their questions sincerely.

Esquivel: How did you reply?

Ikeda: For example, responding to the question about avoiding violence, I said:

> The spirit of rejecting violence is very important. It is noble and great. In addition, you must become strong.
>
> Only cowardly people resort to violence. Because they are actually timid and weak, they try to control others through violence and attack others with brutal words. Those who refuse to resort to violence, however, are actually very strong and brave, so try to become a strong, brave person.

I also stressed that in the struggle for peace one must have a diamond-hard spirit, a heart as strong as a fortress. When I consider that those fourth graders are now all fine young adults, I feel a thrill of excitement.

No matter how times change, there is a way of life and set of values that we must never lose sight of.

Esquivel: I thank you for the constant encouragement you always give to the children and young people of our country.

Ikeda: On the contrary, you and your nation are a constant source of encouragement to our students and young people.

Esquivel: As we said before, globalization and the resulting loss of identities and ethical values are some of the great challenges facing humanity today.

As an educator, I believe we need to reevaluate the content of the education we provide and the values it teaches in the context of the dizzying changes that both our environments and we as human beings are undergoing and the dynamism in the world of thought.

To do this, we must know one another as people and build bridges of cooperation and understanding.

The Secret to the Best Corn

Esquivel: I would like to finish this chapter by sharing a brief but richly suggestive anecdote. I do not know its author, but it was sent to me by the comrades of SERPAJ of Costa Rica, the Red Solidarity.

An enterprising farmer with little education participated in his city's agricultural fair every year. The extraordinary thing was that, year after year, he always won the "Best Corn of the Year" trophy. Each year, he brought his corn to the fair, and each year he walked away with the blue ribbon.

His corn was improving every year. One year a television reporter approached him after he had been presented with yet another blue ribbon. The reporter was eager to learn how it was that he always produced the best corn. He discovered that the farmer shared much of the best seed from his cornfield with his neighbors.

"How can you share your best seeds with your neighbors," the reporter asked, "when they compete directly with you?" "Do you not know why?" asked the farmer in return. "It's simple! The wind carries the pollen from the mature corn and from field to field. If my neighbors cultivated corn inferior to mine, that pollination would continually degrade the quality of my crop. If I want to get good corn, I have to help them grow the best, yielding the best seeds.

"So I hope you can see that we are all important to one another, and that to live well we must help each other. I hope you will also be able to help your neighbors plant the best seeds, the best maize, and the best friendships."

The moral of this little story is that those who choose to be at peace must make their neighbors be at peace. Those who want to live well must help others live well. Those who want to be happy must help others find happiness, because the welfare of each is linked to the well-being of all.

Ikeda: That is a very moving and inspiring story.

It reminds me of the Buddhist teaching: "If one gives food to others, one will improve one's own lot, just as, for example, if one lights a fire for others, one will brighten one's own way."[23]

If I may, I'd like to introduce a Buddhist story that has the same message as the one you just shared. A certain person went to hell. Delicious food was set out before the denizens of hell, but they couldn't eat it because their chopsticks were longer than their arms, and it was impossible for them to place the food in their mouths with such long chopsticks.

Next, the person went to the Buddha land. The chopsticks of the denizens there were also longer than their arms, but they managed to eat to their content. What was different? The denizens of the Buddha land used their long chopsticks to place morsels of food in the mouths of those sitting across and next to them.

This exemplifies the spirit of mutual coexistence that you have spoken of.

The movement being promoted by the SGI in 192 countries and territories around the world is committed to spreading this life of mutual coexistence in one's workplace, community, and society while striving to contribute to peace and prosperity.

THREE

Transmitting the Legacy of Nonviolence

Embracing the Champions of Peace in Our Hearts

Ikeda: The inspiration of the examples of great men and women is a source of tremendous inner strength.

I understand that familiarity from an early age with the writings of people such as Mahatma Gandhi, Leo Tolstoy (1828–1910), and Martin Luther King, Jr., fostered in you respect and admiration for such champions of peace.

I have seen a photograph of you taken at your home next to a statue of Gandhi on the day after the announcement of your receipt of the Nobel Peace Prize in October 1980. I found this a deeply moving testament to the fact that you are also a champion belonging in that great lineage of the human spirit, the philosophy of nonviolence.

Esquivel: It is certainly true that various individuals have had a powerful influence on me. Among them, Mahatma Gandhi stands out as a man who gave up everything in order to be truly human, and he effected tremendous change through his championing of truth and justice.

He served the people. He engaged in social and political actions to promote the people's spiritual awakening, to protect the value of human dignity, and to reaffirm the truth that all human beings are equal and have the same rights.

His nonviolent movement challenged the British Empire. At first it seemed impossible, but through experience and daily struggle, it showed that nonviolent reform can be achieved through opposition and noncooperation—in other words, we can change the prevailing reality through refusal to be complicit with injustice.

Ikeda: I strongly agree. Gandhi's achievement in embodying the Indian spirit of *ahimsa* (not taking life, nonviolence) and reviving it in modern times is one of inexpressible greatness.

As is well known, Albert Einstein (1879–1955) said of Gandhi, "Generations to come, it may be, will scarce believe that such a one as this ever in flesh and blood walked upon this earth."[1]

In my speeches and addresses I have frequently spoken of the significance of Gandhi's thought and actions. My greatest sympathy for Gandhi derives from the fact that he consistently acted among the people, with the people, and for the people. This is attested to by the reflection of his successor Jawaharlal Nehru that Gandhi judged every issue on the basis of the sole criterion of its usefulness to the oppressed people of India.[2]

I also feel a powerful sympathy with Gandhi's limitless belief in the human spirit. This aspect of Gandhi's character can be seen in his fondness for John Ruskin's *Unto This Last*. The title of Ruskin's work is taken from a sentence in the New Testament, which Ruskin (1819–1900) quotes in a poem that opens his book. Ruskin's work inspired Gandhi's powerful personal commitment to seek happiness for all humankind, down to the very last person on Earth.

Gandhi cited the foremost lesson he learned from Ruskin's work as the truth "that the good of the individual is contained in the good of all."[3]

All people, regardless of their social position or economic status, possess a supreme nobility. That is why, as Gandhi's declaration "To serve is my religion"[4] indicates, he focused all his concern on those who were suffering. It is because of that conviction, I believe, that Gandhi chose to spend his life among the people, sharing their joys and sorrows and boldly opposing social ills and all forms of oppression.

Esquivel: I agree completely with your insight.

The Mahatma was an educator. Education was his great objective, which he pursued in the framework of community life, focusing on instilling freedom based on responsibility.

The ashram was the center and ferment of his resistance movement. He said that simply taking India back from the English would be insufficient. The real revolution would not be achieved until the Untouchables had the same rights as the Brahmans.

When asked, he identified the foundation for this struggle and duty as the sacred Indian texts, the Gospels, and the example of Shakyamuni Buddha. As this shows, he was open to the ecumenical spirit and could accept and understand other religions and their truths.

His entire life was an affirmation of prayer and the spiritual path. Gandhi demonstrated through his own example that mystics and contemplatives are active, not passive.

Ikeda: You have noted a very important fact. Faith is conviction. Those whose lives are informed by profound prayer are also deeply committed to justice and their convictions.

Gandhi's life exemplified this continuous struggle of acting while praying and praying while acting. His profound interest in Shakyamuni and Buddhism that you have just noted is well known. For example, in a letter he attested: "I became acquainted with the teaching of the Buddha, my eyes were opened to the limitless possibilities of nonviolence."[5]

He also included the invocation of Nam-myoho-renge-kyo, the phrase expressing the ultimate Law or truth of the universe, in his daily prayers. When I met his grandson Arun Gandhi, he told me that he remembered his grandfather chanting it.

We can see from this that Gandhi was indeed open to Buddhism and other religions. This openness enabled him to transcend the differences among various philosophies and religions and imbibe and sublimate spiritual nourishment from many sources.

Esquivel: Precisely.

Ikeda: I have visited Raj Ghat (in February 1979), where the body of the assassinated Gandhi was cremated. After laying flowers at the memorial, in memory of the noble man who gave his life for the Indian people, I wrote in the visitors' book:

The father of your country sleeps here.
The people of your country visit this shrine.
I pray for the eternal and abundant happiness of
both the father and his children.

At that time, I was thinking of the wish of my mentor Josei Toda, which was expressed in his poem:

To the people of Asia
who pray for a glimpse of the moon
through the parting clouds,
let us send them, instead,
the light of the sun.

Buddhism, which appeared in India through Shakyamuni, was transmitted to Japan after passing through China and the Korean Peninsula. Mr. Toda strongly hoped that the Buddhist philosophy of nonviolence and respect for the dignity of life would now be transmitted from Japan to the land of India, where it would be reborn and illuminate the people like the sun, imparting peace and happiness.

As his disciple, and also with the wish to demonstrate my gratitude to India, the birthplace of Buddhism, I have worked to spread our movement for peace, culture, and education based on the Buddhist philosophy of humanism to India and the rest of Asia.

The Most Significant Figures in Our Lives

Esquivel: Through the struggle of Gandhi and the life paths of the presidents of the Soka Gakkai, I have acquired an understanding of the significance of the mentor and disciple relationship.

At various stages in life, we all look for models to refer to, for spiritual guides and mentors. These may be people in the social, political, and cultural arenas, from the worlds of sport, science, or the arts, or they may be military heroes. They are figures we respect or feel a closeness toward, and our appreciation of their qualities leads us to wish to emulate them. They serve as a source of nourishment for our personal growth and contribute to formulating our identity or view of life.

The first models we have are our parents or others who have raised us. Often we seek great people who, for some reason, have had a strong impact on us. At other times, we discover in other people affirmation or an all-embracing affection that show us the way and guide us along the paths of our lives. The important thing in selecting models is to discover in them values that foster our growth and understanding. When they are physically close at hand, we can engage in person-to-person exchanges that help us gain even deeper understanding. Such people can be considered mentors or spiritual guides.

Encounters with great books can also play a similar role in guiding and inspiring us.

Ikeda: You have raised an important point.

Our lives are shaped by our encounters. In life we have such positive encounters—whether with people or great books—that are sources of tremendous inspiration. They are one of life's great joys.

Esquivel: That is so true. When I was about ten years old, I was a newspaper delivery boy. I often spoke with the many used-book vendors located in the Plaza de Mayo. One of them had an unforgettable effect on me. We were joined by a mysterious bond. He was like an uncle to me.

One day he gave me two books that led to my decision to dedicate my life to justice and peace.

One of the books was *The Seven Storey Mountain* by Thomas Merton (1915–68). Another was Gandhi's *An Autobiography—The Story of My Experiments with Truth.* I avidly consumed Gandhi's autobiography, but Merton's book was too difficult, and I found it heavy going.

I said to my friend: "What on earth are you making me read? I don't understand a word of it!" He replied: "Son, let me tell you how to read it so you understand. First read one chapter. If you don't understand it, just read one page. If you still don't understand it, read one paragraph or one sentence and think about it, think about it deeply, until you understand it. That's the secret to reading."

Ikeda: That is a very heartwarming story. It must be a precious memory.

As a matter of fact, I was also a newspaper delivery boy for three years when I was a similar age to you. I took the job to try to help out, to the best of my ability, with our family's financial difficulties.

No matter what hardships you face, you mustn't become negative or self-pitying. Instead, take action, press onward, even if it's just one step. Overcome the difficulty standing in your path. That was the philosophy I adopted for myself from my boyhood.

Perhaps because of my job delivering newspapers, as a boy I dreamed of becoming a journalist or working in some other capacity as a writer.

I have an unforgettable memory of a young husband and wife, whom I delivered newspapers to. They gave me presents of snacks, and once they invited me to stay for dinner and asked me many questions about my family, encouraging me.

I remember the husband, who was about thirty years old, telling me that the great inventor Thomas Alva Edison (1847–1931) had also delivered newspapers, while keeping up his studies at the same time. He added that people who struggle when they are young are truly fortunate.

But my youth took place during and after the war, when Japanese society was in turmoil, and the circumstances weren't conducive to concentrating on studying. I experienced the misery brought by the war, and I was also battling illness, which prompted me to think deeply about existence and how precious life is. I was eagerly seeking the right way to live, how to lead a good life.

My quest led me to read books filled with the wisdom of humanity. Engaging in a dialogue with the great minds of the past through my reading was a source of tremendous joy for me.

One of the books that nourished me in my youth was *Hyperion* by the German poet Friedrich Hölderlin (1770–1843). In it, he writes: "How fortunate is one who . . . has encountered a noble spirit in his early youth."[6]

Another favorite of my youth was *The Divine Comedy* of Dante Alighieri (1265–1321). In it, Dante says of his joy at departing on a journey with his mentor, the great poet Publius Vergilius Maro (70–19 BCE), "Let us start, for both our wills, joined now, are one. You are my guide, you are my lord and teacher."[7] It is a passage I can never forget.

The greatest joy in my lifetime is having encountered my life's mentor Josei Toda when I was nineteen years old. Nothing is nobler than a life blessed with a great mentor. Even after his death, to this day, I engage in a continuing inner dialogue with Mr. Toda, making it the energy source for my advance day after day.

Has there been anyone of special significance in your life, Dr. Esquivel?

Esquivel: Yes. I can answer your question by relating the following anecdote.

In 2001, I was in Washington, DC to help celebrate the fiftieth anniversary of the Organization of American States (OAS). Among the many people invited to take part were special guests and members of the diplomatic corps, leading authorities, jurists, and representatives of various international organizations.

The day proceeded smoothly, following the established protocols for such events. One of the scheduled activities was a dialogue among five Nobel Laureates from diverse fields, myself included. Audience interest and excitement grew stronger and stronger in the course of sober discussions of the problems of Latin American peoples, human rights, the role of the OAS, and international relations.

The moderator guiding the debate used humor and wit to provide a few moments' diversion and to relax the atmosphere whenever things showed signs of getting too tense. At one of those times, he asked each of us to name his or her most significant hero. Naturally, the question generated expectation and suspense among the audience.

One person cited George Washington (1732–99) and Winston Churchill (1874–1965) for their roles as statesmen committed to the building of the United States of America and Great Britain. Another selected the literary genius and great playwright Shakespeare (1564–1616).

A third designated Marie Curie (1867–1934), who in spite of gender discrimination, courageously demonstrated dedication to science by persisting with her discoveries. A fourth volunteered the name of General Simón Bolívar (1783–1830), the champion of South American independence.

All the people mentioned were extraordinary individuals who had done a great deal for the people and dedicated their lives to carrying out their missions with integrity and humanity. The respondents had named these individuals in recognition of their superior character and contributions to humankind.

Ikeda: All of them were great individuals whose names are inscribed in the annals of human history. Whom did you cite?

Esquivel: When the moderator asked who my hero was, I replied simply, "My Grandmother."

The huge room exploded in laughter. The full diplomatic corps had never laughed so hard. No one had expected me to cite my grandmother as a heroine and momentous figure in my life. I imagine they had expected a more conventional response that was in better accord with social and cultural norms.

But how else could I make the point that there are people who live out their daily lives constructively, despite all sorts of difficulties? How to communicate the fact that there are models for individuals and for society in our own circle of friends and family, in our villages and towns, living out their lives unrecognized and unheralded?

I believe that my answer was right and true. We are all too ready to focus on things grand and far away while overlooking the little things in daily life that are nonetheless just as inspiring and important.

Ikeda: That is very moving. I should like to relate your wonderful response to many of society's leaders.

Once a certain celebrated person asked me what kind of person I considered noblest and greatest. I replied, "Any ordinary mother."

Just as the sun moves through its arc, never halting, in rain or wind, in winter's cold and summer's heat, mothers are continuously fostering, protecting, and compassionately caring for life while shouldering countless burdens.

The lives of ordinary people—those striving out of the limelight and behind the scenes for the welfare of others—are truly noble, shining with sincerity and wisdom and the spirit of service.

I understand that your own mother died when you were only three. Your father, a fisherman, moved from Spain to Argentina looking for a better life. He worked hard, struggling with poverty.

Eventually your siblings were able to go to separate boarding schools, shortly after which you went to live with your maternal grandmother.

She raised you as if she were your Mother Earth.

"Listen to Mother Earth"—A Grandmother's Teaching

Esquivel: That's right. My grandmother Eugenia had a great influence on my attitudes and behavior when I was a boy.

She was of the Guaraní people, and she was strong and vital in spite of her age. She never learned to speak Spanish fluently but preferred to express her feelings in the pleasing Guaraní language. She possessed the sagacity of her people.

She taught me to respect Mother Earth, or *Pachamama* as she is honorifically called, and the wisdom of the Guaraní people. She had a direct awareness of Mother Earth. She talked with animals, plants, and the winds. She could tell when nature was agitated or angered by harm done to her. My ancestors of the Guaraní people preserved in their collective memory the wisdom of their cultural and spiritual roots, and their living history.

My grandmother often said to me, "Come here, son. Sit and let *Pachamama* wrap you in her fragrance. She knows what's good for you. Try to learn to hear her. Don't strain. Just listen to what she says without words."

Ikeda: Your account shows that your grandmother shone with deep humanity, as a philosopher, as a poet.

We human beings must always be humble with regard to nature. If we lose the capacity to listen to the voice of Mother Nature, converse with her, and learn from her, we will lose our very humanity itself.

Buddhism, as one of the foundations of Japanese culture, articulates several important principles for considering the relationship between people and nature. One of them is the doctrine of dependent origination.

"Dependent origination" means "all things occur interdependently." Neither human beings, nature, or indeed anything can exist on its own. They are all the result of causes and conditions, arising in conjunction with and contingent upon one another.

The Indian Buddhist philosopher Nagarjuna (c. 150–250) offers an illustration of the nature of dependent origination in his analysis of fire and fuel appearing in *The Treatise on the Middle Way*.

When we look at wood burning, the fire and the wood are one and cannot be separated from one another. Without the wood, there could be no fire. Likewise, without the fire, the wood would simply be pieces of wood, not the fuel of firewood. In other words, when wood burns, there is no separate fire or separate wood. At the same time, it cannot be said that neither of them exists. The fire exists because of the wood, and the wood exists because of the fire.

In this fashion, all phenomena arise due to dependent origination and are mutually dependent and contingent upon one another.

The Chinese Buddhist scholar Miaole (711–82) formulated this concept of dependent origination as the Buddhist principle of the oneness of life and its environment. Simply put, life and its environment depend upon and are contingent upon one another in their phenomenal aspect. At the same time, from the profound aspect of the ultimate reality of life, the two are one and indivisible.

As a result, harming the natural world is harming human life, in the end.

That's why people like your grandmother, whose lives exemplify a model of respect for nature, are deserving of recognition. Can you tell me more about your grandmother?

Esquivel: My grandmother Eugenia was a countrywoman accustomed to the sun and to hard work. Long years of strenuous labor had made her hands strong and weathered. The deep wrinkles on her face were marks of time.

When seated alone, she seemed to be waiting and listening in the silence. Her deep, weary, black eyes observed everything around her.

She knew how to make wise deductions from human behavior. Years gave her the ability to understand without words. We used to say that she had a keen nose for people. She was rarely mistaken in evaluating people and was able to immediately spot the arrogant and proud. She easily exposed people who, like actors, played a part and, confident in their ability to conceal their own identity behind a facade, hoped that others would notice only the performance.

Ikeda: You refer to people who wear a false mask.

Esquivel: That's right. In her limited Spanish vocabulary she would say things like, "That's a good person, she knows how to look at you and listen to you."

When she disliked someone, she would say, "Watch out for him. He doesn't look you in the eye. He's ready to claw you at any moment." She would offer such vivid, easily comprehensible images to warn us. She also said: "Never trust anybody who won't look you in the eye and who beats around the bush when saying something he doesn't want to say."

In our lives we all have unforgettable people who remain in our spirits permanently, in spite of the passage of time and the separation of distance.

Ikeda: Your profound respect and admiration for your grandmother is clearly evident.

She certainly seems to have been very perceptive about people. If all the ordinary people were to become as wise as your grandmother, they would easily see through the arrogant and those of malicious intent. They would no longer be deceived and harmed by bad leaders.

The people must become wiser. They must acquire more strength to create an age in which the people exercise decisive influence over leaders in government and society. And if leaders do not commune and interact with the people, familiarizing themselves with their thoughts, deep-seated concerns, and aspirations, they will be unable to lead our turbulent, constantly changing society to prosperity and victory.

The people are a goal in themselves; they must never be regarded as a mere means. They are the focal point. Putting people in the center of our thinking is the way to find hints for solutions to the various problems of our times.

The Pioneers of the Nonviolent Movement in Latin America

Esquivel: I agree wholeheartedly.

In addition to my grandmother, I might mention another who inspired me and set me an example, the Italian mystic, philosopher, author, and disciple of Mahatma Gandhi, Lanza del Vasto (1901–81).

Vasto journeyed to India to participate in the independence campaign, working with Vinoba Bhave (1895–1982), one of Gandhi's chosen disciples. Bhave was involved with the agrarian reform movement called Land Gift.

Vasto discovered in the activities of daily life the social and spiritual dimensions of nonviolence as a liberating force. His numerous written works include *Peregrinación a las Fuentes* (Return to the Source) and *Judas*. Upon returning to Europe, he founded the Community of the Ark, a religious, ecumenical, working order based on the Gandhian ashram.

I met him at a conference on nonviolence at the Faculty of Law of the University of Buenos Aires when I was still very young. His lecture helped awaken me to new social dimensions and ideas. We became friends, and my wife and son and I decided to join the Community of the Ark. We took part in the first nonviolent demonstrations held in Argentina and thereafter in various Latin American countries.

Ikeda: So that's how you began your social activism. Gandhi's disciples gathered from around the world, took part in activities under

Gandhi's guidance, and then went off to other places around the globe to carry on the struggle.

Vinoba Bhave is famous as one of Gandhi's leading spiritual heirs. He was the leader of Gandhi's *Sarvodaya* (welfare of all) movement. The agricultural reform movement he initiated, "Land Gift" (Bhoodan Yajna), convinced thousands of landowners to donate some of their holdings to the landless.

How did he achieve this seemingly impossible feat? When we discussed the reasons for the success of this difficult undertaking, Dr. Neelakanta Radhakrishnan, a former director of the Gandhi Smiriti and Darshan Samiti (Gandhi Memorial Hall) in New Delhi, described Bhave's method: "His compassionate approach to problems confronting his fellow human beings was marked by an openness to others' views. He always encouraged dialogue among the various schools of thought to which many of his followers belonged."[8]

A man of noble character, Bhave was a master at inspiring people through dialogue brimming with conviction.

Are there others who have exerted a strong influence on your life?

Esquivel: Others whom I must mention as having influenced my life and destiny are a married couple: the Austrian theologian Hildegard Goss-Mayr and Jean Goss (1912–91), a French hero of World War II. Having witnessed atrocities committed during the war in Algeria by French soldiers carrying out government orders, Jean Goss decided to return all the war decorations conferred on him by the French government. Then, as nonviolent activists, the pair traveled to places like Africa and the Middle East promoting the training of activists dedicated to nonviolence as a force for liberation.

They were the first to initiate nonviolent movements in Latin America in an organized fashion. In 1962, they started traveling the continent visiting religious leaders and bishops, social organizations, labor unions, and other groups to inform and educate leaders capable of undertaking nonviolent actions.

Their task was not an easy one. At a time of violent movements such as the Cuban Revolution and guerrilla activities in Colombia, Jean Goss was arguing in earnest for the need for nonviolent struggles. The couple worked with equal enthusiasm in Brazil and Mexico too, and the fruit of their labor was the emergence of bishops like Dom Hélder Pessoa Câmara (1909–99) and Dom Antônio Batista Fragoso (1920–2006) in Brazil, and numerous other supporters to participate in nonviolent actions.

In its later years, the movement expanded to the point where, in February 1974, member groups held an international conference in the Colombian city of Medellín. Acting on a decision of this assembly, I undertook the formation of an organization that was to become SERPAJ in Latin America.

Ikeda: That is very important historical background.

Gandhi, too, expended tremendous effort proclaiming and propagating the philosophy of nonviolence. He famously wrote, "Every good movement passes through five stages: indifference, ridicule, abuse, repression, and respect."[9]

As we consider their achievements, Hildegard Goss-Mayr and Jean Goss and their fellow workers have my greatest respect for their pioneering work in South America.

Gandhi Assigns a Young Brahman Disciple to Clean Toilets

Ikeda: The nonviolent movement is at once a spiritual struggle and an educational movement setting out to reform human minds fundamentally.

In this connection, I am reminded of the experiences of my respected friend and one of Gandhi's preeminent disciples, Dr. B. N. Pande (1906–98), whom I have met both in India and in Tokyo.

Joining Gandhi in 1921, Pande devoted himself completely to the nonviolent movement. Because of this work, he was imprisoned eight times for a total of ten years. He was a person of great serenity, under which could be perceived an unbendable will forged through years of struggle.

He recounted to me his first meeting with Gandhi, which took place when he was only fourteen.

Gandhi asked him whether he was a Brahman.

When Pande replied affirmatively, Gandhi said, "In the ashram, the Brahmans are allotted a particular type of work. Will you do it?" Pande responded that he would.

The job Gandhi assigned him was cleaning toilets. In India, Brahmans, the highest Hindu caste, would never do this task, which was relegated to the lowest caste. Nevertheless, the youth cleaned the toilets every day. In the morning he prepared night-soil fertilizer for the fields. In the afternoon, he spun thread with a traditional spinning wheel or *charkha* and wove clothes.

Dr. Pande reflected that he only realized later how correct Gandhi had been in giving him this kind of work to do. If he was to be champion of nonviolence, he had to rid himself of the sense of superiority he felt as a Brahman. By doing lowly work such as cleaning communal toilets and collecting trash, he was able to abandon his sense of superiority and become one with the others there. As Gandhi often said, his aim was building a nation of equality in which everyone is important.

Gandhi used everyday activities to teach human dignity and equality and to educate champions of nonviolence one by one.

Esquivel: That is a very illuminating story. All the people whom I have mentioned as significant in my life were also always consistent in word and deed. Spirituality was the axis that gave meaning to their lives. They were never distracted by easy triumphs, vanity, or arrogance. Their goal was to share the life of the people and to walk side by side with the poorest sectors of society.

They humbly faced the historical challenges of their times with social, cultural, and political commitment. Through popular organizations, they sought paths to liberation for the ordinary people and found ways that would allow the poorest to become the protagonists in their own lives. They were all great educators capable of awakening a critical spirit and creating new spaces of freedom.

In your writings, you explain that the spirit of Mahayana Buddhism is embodied in the bodhisattva's way of life, "seeking enlightenment above and saving living beings below."[10] That phrase perfectly describes the spirit of the people I have been discussing.

Ikeda: No matter how elevated the religion, it is those who practice it who are most important. No matter what philosophy or system of thought we subscribe to, and however skillfully we interpret it, it is worthless if we cannot put its content into practice in our daily lives.

As you have just noted, Mahayana Buddhism stresses that one's own enlightenment—that is, self-realization and happiness—is attained through the practice of the bodhisattva to help all living beings attain enlightenment.

In his *Treatise on the Great Perfection of Wisdom,* Nagarjuna describes the nature of the bodhisattva as follows:

> Because the mind of the bodhisattva benefits both self and others, because he enables all living beings to attain enlightenment, because he knows the true nature of all dharmas (things, phenomena), because he practices the path to supreme perfect enlightenment, and because he is praised by all worthies and sages, he is called a bodhisattva.[11]

The bodhisattva embodies a noble way of life as a human being.

Following this passage, the *Treatise on the Great Perfection of Wisdom* states: "For the sake of all living beings, he pursues the Buddhist way to attain liberation from birth, aging, and death, and is therefore called a bodhisattva."[12]

The most important means for liberating people from suffering and enabling them to attain enlightenment are the "weapons" of nonviolence—words and dialogue.

The Dangerous Gap between Words and Deeds

Esquivel: The word is the energy that transmits thoughts, but when the thoughts are communicated and apprehended, the essence of the energy subsists and the transmitting word disappears. Written words, however, retain their power over time and are etched in the collective consciousness and in the history of the people as a part of their shared memory. The word in its various manifestations through the arts records human events great and small, joyous and tragic, and documents the spirituality and identity of the people.

Precisely because words have such power, the insight of the Chinese Daoist philosopher Zhuangzi (Chuang Tzu, late fourth century BCE) deserves our attention:

> The fish trap exists because of the fish; once you've gotten the fish, you can forget the trap. The rabbit snare exists because of the rabbit; once you've gotten the rabbit, you can forget the snare. Words exist because of meaning; once you've gotten the meaning, you can forget the words. Where can I find a man who has forgotten words so I can have a word with him?[13]

Ikeda: In the famous passage you mention, Zhuangzi comments on the folly of focusing solely on superficial verbal and literary forms and overlooking the essential meanings behind them.

By "meaning," he refers to the essence or truth of a thing—what you have called the energy that transmits the thought, that is, the spirit. Words are important because they transmit this spirit from person to person and over the ages. We must not, however, become so obsessed with words that we lose sight of their inner spirit. That is what Zhuangzi is saying, I believe.

Buddhism explains the relation between verbal expressions and their inner meanings through the principle of text, meaning, and intent. The vast Buddhist canon, often referred to as the eighty thousand teachings, is comprised of an enormous number of scriptures, or sutras. "Text" refers to a sutra's literal content, while "meaning" indicates the doctrines or principles to which the text refers. "Intent" indicates the deeper level of the text's heart or essential intent.

Zhiyi (538–97), the founder of Tiantai Buddhism in China, and Nichiren in Japan regarded the Lotus Sutra as the scripture presenting the true content of Shakyamuni's enlightenment. A superficial reading of the text of the sutra, however, will not reveal that enlightenment. We must delve deeper, transcending the meaning of the teachings presented in the sutra and arriving at and experientially grasping the intent they express.

To apprehend the profound intent, the truth of enlightenment, we need to not only read the text and study the meaning of the teachings but, crucially, engage in the practice of the bodhisattva way. Only through carrying out our human revolution, in which we break free from the lesser self and achieve the greater self in sympathy with others, through Buddhist practice, does the intent (truth) in the depths of the sutra become clear. Action is crucial.

Esquivel: I think so, too. Spirituality is born when we are able to open our minds and hearts to create inner space that allows light to enter. It comes into being when the spirit unites with the transcendence of the One in all things. No one can give what he or she doesn't have.

To achieve peace, we need a spirituality that illuminates our self— an inner light. Without that light, we cannot illuminate others.

To paraphrase Zhuangzi, "Where can I find a man or woman who has forgotten the word 'peace'? I should like to talk with such a man or woman."

Ikeda: That is very true. No amount of talking about peace will make it a reality. The spirit and power of peace pulsate in concrete efforts to promote respect for human worth and dignity, in building strong solidarity among people.

You touched on this point in the speech you made in November 1996, at the Boston Research Center for the 21st Century (the present Ikeda Center for Peace, Learning, and Dialogue), on the occasion of receiving the Global Citizen Award.

Perceptively identifying the problems facing modern society, you said that politicians have lost their sense of ethics and society's leaders their spirituality. As economic values have hypertrophied, human values and our sense of identity have been sacrificed. The home has been reduced to little more than a shelter, when in fact it should be a means for enriching our lives.

You went on to say that so far you had portrayed a very grave future, but we also have to focus on the signs of hope that exist. As people, you said, we cannot be mere spectators. We have to become the protagonists of our history. We have to learn to unite in the building of a culture of solidarity and hope. You added that instead of lamenting the absence of ideals, we must bring forth our own ideals. If we want freedom, we must struggle against the forces that repress freedom. Retreat and resignation are evil. You concluded that peace is something that must be won, and it will be won only through struggle.

When you said that peace will not come to those who sit and wait, that it must be won, you affirmed my own conviction born of many years of participation in the pacifist movement.

Esquivel: We constantly hear much fine talk about peace and human rights in majestic ceremonies and at conventions where treaties and protocols are ratified. The nations' leaders applaud each speech, promising to comply with and execute the things they sign. But the majority of them do not believe in what they are saying and applauding. This is the attitude of many political leaders, scientists, and educators. They have lost their passion and commitment to peace and make no effort to match their deeds to their words.

They have forgotten that peace is the dynamic that gives meaning and life to humanity. They have stripped it of content and proclaim, "If you want peace, prepare for war." And they raise the terror of the nuclear holocaust as a guarantee of peace.

Ikeda: War treats human life as no more than a tool. In contrast, peace is created when we safeguard life and protect human rights, making the dignity of life our ultimate goal. It is for these purposes that all social institutions—political and educational—exist. I am convinced that to value anything other than life or more than life is to oppress humanity.

As you point out, humanity is often sacrificed to the interests of politics and the economy, which ought to exist solely as the means to produce and protect human happiness. We must correct this reversal of priorities, this vicious cycle.

This reversal of priorities has been caused by the widespread prevalence of people leading completely self-centered lives, perfectly willing to sacrifice others for their own power and profit. That is why in my proposals and speeches at educational institutions around the world I ardently advocate for the opposite way of life: the principle of not building one's own happiness on the misfortune of others.

Esquivel: That is a moral principle that we would all do well to remember and apply on a daily basis.

We live in a world convulsed by violence and conflicts of various origins, with competition prevailing over solidarity and economic interests predominating over the interests of human beings. Our societies are focused solely on the demands of the marketplace, while completely forgetting the needs of the poorest people.

Countries with serious problems, plagued by the fearsome "silent bomb" of famine, spend billions of dollars on nuclear weapons—for example, Pakistan and, paradoxically, India, the land of Gandhi.

Gandhi taught nonviolence as the fundamental principle of spiritual and social life. Through nonviolence, fighting for the people and embodying a model for life, he opposed the British Empire and showed his people the way to peace. He did not limit himself to political and social action; he deepened education in the villages or ashram to instill the values of peace in the minds and in the actual attitudes of each human being toward their life.

Yet while national leaders and officials have promised to preserve and strengthen peace, we see people fighting among themselves in seemingly unresolvable conflicts—conflicts orchestrated and exacerbated by those very leaders and governments.

Unless our leaders have peace in their hearts, minds, and spirits, peace will never be established on Earth.

The power of domination is like the spell a serpent casts to hypnotize its victim before striking with its venom. The majority of governments are incapable of resisting the spell of power.

Reaching Peace on the Path to Spirituality

Ikeda: I am reminded of a warning Gandhi once delivered to a certain political leader: "Beware of power; power corrupts. Do not let yourselves be entrapped by its pomp and pageantry. Remember, you are in office to serve the poor in India's villages."[14]

In our earlier discussion, I remarked that Buddhism identifies the evil of power with what is called the life force of the devil king of the sixth heaven. In the worldview of Buddhism, the sixth heaven is the highest realm in the world of desire.[15] It is also known as the Heaven of Freely Enjoying Things Conjured by Others, meaning that it is a realm where beings can freely dominate and exploit others for their own selfish interests. In other words, the realm represents the egoism that is a fundamental part of life. It represents a state in which in spite of satisfying all our material cravings and social ambitions, we are driven to constantly seek more, becoming slaves to our desires.

The Heaven of Freely Enjoying Things Conjured by Others is manifested as a life state in people who are driven to use their wealth and power to dominate others with impunity. They rob others of their respect as human beings and reduce them to a means to gratify their own greed. Those in power are always susceptible to becoming driven by the pathology of inhumanity. As a result, struggling for the dignity of human life is necessarily a struggle against this devilish aspect of power. We can never fail in our vigilance in monitoring those who wield power and authority.

The US civil rights leader Dr. Martin Luther King, Jr., in spite of being incarcerated, kept up his struggle against power and urged his followers to fight relentlessly: "If history teaches anything, it is that evil is recalcitrant and determined, and never voluntarily relinquishes its hold short of an almost fanatical resistance. Evil must be attacked by a counteracting persistence, by the day-to-day assault of the battering rams of justice."[16]

Esquivel: Exactly. That greed for power and domination you describe is the source of all human suffering. We need to reflect on the conditions prevailing in our societies. Today more than fifty wars and conflicts are taking place in different places on this little planet of ours. Each of us, men and women, who inhabit this world that is our communal home need to rediscover ourselves spiritually. Lost in power and violence, we are exhausted in a mad race to nowhere.

We must return to the ways of the spirit that lead us to peace.

Ikeda: How can we change our world, racked by constant violence and war? As you say, the key is for the people to join together in solidarity through profound spirituality. With that solidarity, we must circumscribe, monitor, and correct the evil nature of power.

I also believe that it is crucial for those in power to rediscover a profound religiosity and spirituality.

Gandhi repeatedly declared concerning the relationship between politics and religion: "For me, politics bereft of religion are absolute dirt, ever to be shunned."[17] He also said: "My struggle is not merely political. It is religious and therefore quite pure."[18]

Power holders need a sound religiosity and spirituality if they are to triumph over evil, purify their life force, and correct their actions. This is the basic significance of Gandhi's declaration.

FOUR

Women: The Driving Force of a Century of Life

Building Solidarity in an Individualistic Society

Ikeda: Many, including myself, see women as playing the leading role in the third millennium that has begun with the arrival of the twenty-first century. Women are characterized by their loving, compassionate nurturing of life.

Today all organizations and societies will find it hard to grow and evolve unless they respect the wisdom of women and value their input much more than they have in the past. The failure to do so places the future in jeopardy and could even result in society advancing once again along the dreadful path of war.

Women have the ability to transform human history, bringing about a shift from an era of war and violence to one of peace and harmonious coexistence. A network of women working for good is the very foundation of the peace and happiness of the human race.

In the SGI, women are engaged in wonderful activities to build a culture of peace in 192 countries and territories. As an example, in Argentina in April 2007, the SGI-Argentina Committee of Women for Peace was established and held its first conference at the SGI-Argentina Peace Auditorium in Buenos Aires.

I would like to thank you for accepting the position of honorary president of the committee. Your wife, Amanda Guerreño, attended that first conference. You were not in Argentina at the time, but you sent an inspiring message, which she read aloud on your behalf during the proceedings. I would once again like to express my gratitude for your deeply meaningful contribution, which I know made a profound impression on all the participants.

Esquivel: It is an honor for me. Unfortunately, as I was in the Basque region of Spain supporting interethnic peace and understanding, I was unable to attend the conference. Nonetheless, I am honored to have been able to play even a small part.

In my message I had the following to say about the struggle being waged by you and all SGI members:

> In his work as the president of the SGI, Mr. Ikeda has dedicated his life to illuminating humanity with the light of understanding and fostering an awareness of all the issues facing humankind. Everything SGI members can do for the good of their community is a good for the human race. That is why I am sure that the women of your organization, sensitive and concerned, are working to leave to their children and future generations a more just and amicable world.

The conference you mention was followed by an environmental exhibition entitled "Seeds of Change: The Earth Charter and Human Potential," the content of which I understand was very rewarding and fruitful.

How can we create a culture of solidarity in modern society, which is growing increasingly individualistic? The only way is for everyone, not just women, to actively address social diversity and attempt to extract solidarity from it.

In this sense, I expect great things from the wholehearted actions of SGI members, who transcend divisive differences, build bridges among diverse cultures, and demonstrate the potential for embracing and including those differences in actual daily affairs.

Gandhi's High Hopes for the Role of Women

Ikeda: Thank you for your warm words of understanding and encouragement concerning the initiatives we are undertaking as a movement for peace. I deeply appreciate your support and cooperation. Our great hope is that our movement can provide the seeds of reform necessary to cope with global warming and the other grave issues confronting humanity.

At the same time the SGI-Argentina Committee of Women for Peace was holding its conference in April 2007, the Institute of Oriental Philosophy on the campus of Soka University in Tokyo was co-sponsoring an Indo-Japan Joint Symposium to commemorate the Centennial of Gandhi's Satyagraha.

During the symposium, my great friend Dr. N. Radhakrishnan stressed the degree of trust that Mahatma Gandhi placed in the power of women, noting that Gandhi can be regarded as the first person in history to assign women roles in an important social movement. He did not measure the wealth of a country in terms of glorious architecture or powerful weaponry but instead saw women, who care for and foster life, as a society's greatest treasure, said Dr. Radhakrishnan. He believed that a country that does not respect its women has no future.[1]

I strongly agree with that position.

Esquivel: I agree with him, too.

Some years ago on a visit to Mumbai I met men and women who fought beside Gandhi in the struggle for Indian independence. Though already of advanced age, they preserved their ideals and their passion for the nonviolent resistance movement.

Gandhi knew that men and women had to share the road to independence under equal conditions. A large number of those still keeping alight the flame of ideals of liberty they had lit together with Gandhi were women.

About the potential of women, Gandhi said: "If by strength is meant brute strength, then indeed is woman less brute than man. If by strength is meant moral power, then woman is immeasurably man's superior. If non-violence is the law of our being, the future is with woman."[2]

Ikeda: Those are famous words. One of the courageous women who took part in Gandhi's movement was Usha Mehta (1920–2000), former director of the Gandhi Memorial Hall (Mani Bhavan Gandhi Sangrahalaya).

Together with Usha Gokani, Gandhi's granddaughter, Dr. Mehta twice welcomed groups from the Soka Gakkai youth division to India (in 1992 and 1994).

Her first meeting with Gandhi occurred when she was just eight years old. After enduring four years in prison during the independence struggle, she went on to faithfully transmit his spirit for the rest of her life.

She described what she learned from Gandhi as follows:

Gandhi taught us this: "Fight courageously for what is right. Speak the truth" and "By establishing peace in the hearts of women, you will establish a peaceful society. At that time, the peaceful power of women will become a great and explosive force that will change society."[3]

Dr. Mehta also encouraged the Soka Gakkai youth visiting India, saying: "When you enter the Gandhi Memorial Hall you are guests, but when you depart you are comrades. Let us join hands and, as members of the Mahatma Gandhi's expanded family, follow the path of peace, and carry on our struggle!"

It cannot be denied that throughout history the masculine perspective has dominated while the true greatness and the power of women's courage have been underestimated. I believe, however, that women, refusing to countenance political oppression and injustice, have played the central role in making a fresh breakthrough in history through the power of the spirit.

Women Who Have Dedicated Their Lives to the Struggle for Justice

Esquivel: Yes, women who have sacrificed themselves in the struggle for life and liberty have demonstrated immeasurable courage and dignity. They have created models that all humanity should recognize and appreciate. Indubitably, no force can inspire and motivate people as strongly as the courage of a woman aflame with justice, irrepressibly crying out for liberty.

Women have always played a leading, constructive role in the long history of social, political, and cultural activism in Latin America and many other parts of the world. Many of them have left marks on the lives of their peoples.

It is hard to enumerate all of the ones who have exerted an influence over that long span of history, but one notable representative was Rosa Parks (1913–2005), mother of the civil rights movement in the United States.

Ikeda: I had the deepest respect and admiration for Rosa Parks, who, sadly, died in October 2005. I met her on two occasions: in 1993 on the then Soka University Los Angeles campus in Calabasas and a year later at Soka University in Tokyo.

I shall always remember how much pleasure she derived from meeting our young students. She told them of the historic Montgomery Bus Boycott (1955–56) that she herself ignited. As you know, the city of Montgomery, Alabama had a regulation requiring black bus riders to sit in the segregated section in the rear and to give up their seats in the unreserved section to white people when rows for whites became full.

But her mother had taught her the importance of firmly maintaining her self-respect. Returning from work on December 1, 1955, she boarded a bus and sat in the unreserved section. When a white passenger later got on, the driver ordered her to move to the rear.

She flatly refused. She described her feelings at the time to our Soka students, saying: "I felt I could no longer bear to silently submit to the discrimination I had endured for so many years. I was arrested and jailed. I had no idea how many other black Americans would rise up in protest against my treatment, and no notion of the persecution I might be subjected to, but I was prepared to take whatever came my way."[4]

Esquivel: Rosa Parks felt the need to cry, "Enough!" She stood up to fight against what she knew to be wrong and take part in the civil disobedience movement, which spurred the bus boycott movement against the injustice of racial discrimination.

Her courageous "No" initiated a resistance movement of which Martin Luther King, Jr., was later to take the lead, and which was to result in the passing of civil rights legislation in 1964.

Today there are many Rosa Parkses in the world. Indeed, there is one in every person.

Ikeda: I have the same impression. Her declaration has a universal greatness. Her words reveal the fundamental conclusion she arrived at through her struggle: "I have learned that in order to bring about change, one must not be afraid to take the first step, or else it will not be done. I believe that the only failure is failing to try."[5]

Many women have unquestionably inherited her spirit and courage. In the struggle for human rights, Nadine Gordimer (1923–2014), who fought against apartheid in South Africa, and Rigoberta Menchú Tum from Guatemala are examples of women who have opposed violence with the power of the human spirit.

Innumerable women are standing in the lead of such struggles around the world, speaking out for justice.

Esquivel: That is an extremely timely observation. There are indeed women pointing out the way and bearing witness to the possibility of resistance to all humanity, and 1992 Nobel Peace Prize laureate Rigoberta Menchú Tum is one of them.

I know of the struggle she has been engaged in since her youth, when her own family was massacred and she fled to Mexico (in 1981). With great courage she denounced the military dictatorship in Guatemala. She has made her voice calling for an end to violence and massacres heard around the world.

Ikeda: I have great admiration for her resolute struggle for human rights.

As you have stated, she is a great Guatemalan leader who has striven tirelessly at the risk of her life in the fight to improve the status of the indigenous peoples and to establish their basic human rights. She has traveled around the world as a Goodwill Ambassador for the United Nations ever since the International Year of the World's Indigenous People (1993).

The essence of greatness as a human being is transforming one's own deepest sufferings into the power to fight for the happiness of others. She has said: "There are no national boundaries in the struggle for human rights. What matters is the feeling one has for our common humanity and for life."[6]

The shining light of respect for the worth of human beings and life is irrefutably evident in the noble actions of this woman fighting for human rights and to preserve life. Nichiren writes in one of his treatises: "Here a single individual has been used as an example, but the same thing applies equally to all living beings."[7]

Rigoberta Menchú Tum, you, and I were among the fifty-five people from all over the world who signed the Appeal to End the

Nuclear Weapons Threat to Humanity published in *The New York Times* in 2000 (April 24).

Esquivel: It was a splendid joint effort indeed. But I would also like to speak a little about another great female champion of human rights, the Myanmar leader Aung San Suu Kyi.

I traveled with a group of Nobel laureates to try to visit her in Myanmar by way of Thailand in order to show our support for her. The group included Archbishop Desmond Tutu from the Republic of South Africa and two brave Irish fighters—Betty Williams, WCCI founder and president, and Mairead Corrigan Maguire—who, as everyone knows, engaged in peaceful resistance to the violence unleashed by the Irish Republican Army and the British Army. The military dictatorship of Myanmar, however, denied us permission to enter the country.

Ikeda: On the occasion of the sixtieth birthday of Aung San Suu Kyi in June 2005, a group of Nobel Peace Prize laureates, including you, Betty Williams, and president emeritus of the Pugwash Conferences Joseph Rotblat (1908–2005), published an open letter to her.

In November 2006, Betty Williams and I met in Tokyo to discuss women's role in achieving peace and how to break the vicious cycle of violence.

In 1976, during the storm of violence that swept Northern Ireland, she experienced the horror of witnessing three innocent children killed in front of their mother. This tragedy inspired her to rise up in anger.

"I got angry, really angry," she recalled, "and I've never lost that anger. Anger can be a very destructive emotion if you allow it to be, but it can also be very creative."

The rage Dr. Williams experienced at witnessing the cruel violence that took the lives of the children right before her eyes transformed her into a warrior for peace. As Nichiren wrote: "From this you should understand that anger can be either a good or a bad thing."[8]

Anger consumed by selfish greed is evil, but anger against evil and for justice is good.

Esquivel: As you say, nothing is as powerful as the anger and outrage of women at injustice. Awakened by the life-shaking tragedy of losing their beloved sons and daughters, they deliver a heartbreaking cry issuing from the depths of their beings. There are many such women. The resistance movement was born from the innermost depths of women, who initiated a struggle to protect human worth and dignity.

The social demonstrations of mothers, grandmothers, and families gathering in the Plaza de Mayo in Argentina were born of just such a cry.

Similarly, women demonstrated great courage in the civil war in El Salvador (1980–92) as well as showing remarkable courage and resistance in the midst of the harsh repression perpetrated by the military dictatorship against the Guatemalan people. Their persistence motivated many women in Europe, the United States, Canada, and numerous parts of Latin America to gather, unite, and take action to support the people, willing to risk their own lives to save the lives of others.

Mothers' Prayers: The Starting Point for Action for Peace

Ikeda: As we have discussed previously, during the military dictatorship of the 1970s in Argentina, many people were suddenly carried off from their homes at gunpoint by military personnel and "disappeared." Beloved children and spouses suddenly went missing, never to return. With your leadership and support, surviving mothers, grandmothers, and other family members formed the movement called the Mothers of the Plaza de Mayo.

You were one of the first to voice your solidarity with these Mothers and Grandmothers of the Plaza de Mayo. As of 2009, some thirty years have passed since the start of this movement, with its famous marches and demonstrations, which took the form of walking in a circle.

Esquivel: Indeed, I supported them from the beginning. Starting in 1977, every Thursday mothers with their heads covered by white scarves assembled in the plaza. The names of disappeared family members were embroidered in blue on headscarves; their photographs hung from the women's necks. Gradually the numbers of demonstrators increased. But the majority of their loved ones were tortured and killed in detention centers, never to return to their homes even after the government's transition from military dictatorship to democracy.

I still cannot stop thinking about the sight of these loving Mothers of the Plaza de Mayo. The cry of these mothers who had lost their children was, "Our children gave birth to us"; they continue their fight against wrongs and injustice to this day.

Ikeda: That's a deeply moving story.

When I was in your country in February 1993, I made a courtesy visit to the Palace of the Argentina National Congress, and at that time I drove by the Plaza de Mayo. I still vividly remember my impression at seeing from the car the "battleground" where Argentine women engaged in such a courageous struggle for respect for human life.

Esquivel: Indeed, for these women the Plaza de Mayo was like a battleground.

Women's movements fighting for human rights, like the Mothers of the Plaza, are arising powerfully around the world.

In 2000, after the Gulf War (1990–91), I visited Iraq in the company of 1976 Nobel Peace laureate Mairead Corrigan Maguire, representatives of the International Fellowship of Reconciliation, which is headquartered in the Netherlands, and American peace groups.

We arrived in Baghdad after a thousand-mile desert crossing from Amman in Jordan. Awaiting us was a woman covered head to foot in traditional black robes and wearing a black hijab covering her head.

Her name was Ayamira, and she lived in a wagon parked in front of a children's refuge that had been bombed by American and British forces, taking the lives of six hundred children and their mothers. Ayamira escaped because she had been washing her children's clothing some distance from the shelter. When she returned, she found her whole family dead. They had died inside the shelter.

This quiet woman was eloquent testimony to a people struggling to recover its values and identity.

Ikeda: It is said that 90 percent of the victims of armed conflict are innocent civilians, of which the majority are women and children.

Throughout humanity's long history, a staggering number of mothers have died in conflict and war, or been reduced to grief-stricken misery at the loss of their beloved children or husbands.

I have personally experienced the tragedy of war, so I know. As I mentioned earlier, I watched our house being burned to ashes in an air raid, feeling utterly helpless to prevent it. As was the case with many families at that time, we were forcibly evacuated from our home by the government. When we were finally able to build a new house on some land owned by relatives, it too was burned to the ground in an air raid. Our only resort was to erect a sort of barracks-style hut on the ruins.

Even worse was the loss of my oldest brother, who had been drafted to fight in World War II. A year or two after the war's end, three of my four brothers who had been sent to the battlefields returned home alive, but my oldest brother never returned. One day we received an official telegram informing us that he had died in battle in Burma (present-day Myanmar).

I still remember my mother's overpowering grief when she received the news. She was an optimistic and hardworking person, and I'm sure this was the saddest event in her entire life.

Once during the war we spent the entire night in an air raid shelter during a B-29 attack. At dawn, after the bombers had gone, an American soldier whose plane must have been hit by anti-aircraft fire parachuted to the ground. I saw his face close-up as he came down. He was a blond youth, still possessing boyish features and probably around twenty years of age.

We Japanese at that time were indoctrinated to think of all American and British people as devils and brutes, so as soon as the youth hit the ground local citizens surrounded him and beat him severely with sticks, until finally the Japanese military police led him away. When I told my mother about this after I returned home she said, "Poor boy! His mother must be worried to death about him."

My mother's reaction etched in my innermost being just how cruel and brutal, how foolhardy war is, inflicting such suffering and sadness on mothers around the world.

There are no borders separating the hearts of mothers, the givers and caretakers of life. There are no barriers or distinctions of race in them.

The lesson I learned from my mother's silent grief at the news of my brother's death is one of the starting points of my actions for peace to this day.

Esquivel: In other words, the starting point of your courageous actions for peace is your deep feelings for your mother, and likewise, toward all the mothers of the world.

Women Illuminating Society with the Light of Compassion

Esquivel: The millennium opened with great violence and numerous armed conflicts, as exemplified by the events in Afghanistan and Iraq.

As has been the case in the conflict in the African Great Lakes Region, war claims more victims among women and children than among soldiers. More than three million people have been killed in the genocide in that region, which was ignored by the mass media.

Violent conflicts are also underway in Colombia, several countries of Latin America, and elsewhere around the world, but in all these bloody scenarios, a common feature is the presence of women. Many of them have fallen victim to the fire, but others stand out as active participants in the resistance, or as dedicated to building more just and humane societies. They are simply there, with their presence and their testimony to life. They are people with faces, voices, and names, illuminating a new way forward for us.

Ikeda: They are remarkable. Women who have survived an age of war are noble exemplars demonstrating the possibility of transforming adversity into mission.

Buddhism teaches the principle of "voluntarily assuming the appropriate karma."[9] In other words, to alleviate the sufferings of living beings, bodhisattvas choose to be born in this evil, corrupt world and, enduring the suffering and hardship of that world, fight tirelessly to help other beings.

All people have a hometown and a homeland. They live within a community, a society. When they courageously stand up and make an earnest effort to improve the environment inextricably connected to their lives and follow through in their own way in doing what they believe to be right and good, striving to produce results attesting to their work, they transform their karma into mission. In this action a tested and true humanity shines.

This superior capacity for community involvement and contribution is a trait that seems to be more commonly seen in women than men.

You have noted that the disaster of armed conflict takes its heaviest toll on women and children. In that connection, I might cite the praise of women that Richard von Weizsäcker (1920–2015), philosopher and first president of the unified postwar Germany, offered in a famous speech commemorating the fortieth anniversary of the end of World War II:

Perhaps the greatest burden was borne by the women of all nations. Their suffering, renunciation and silent strength are all too easily forgotten by history. Filled with fear, they worked, bore human life and protected it. They mourned their fallen fathers and sons, husbands, brothers and friends. In the years of darkness, they ensured that the light of humanity was not extinguished. After the war, with no prospect of a secure future, women everywhere were the first to set about building homes again.[10]

In the darkest times, women have demonstrated immeasurable strength in protecting the light of humanity.

Esquivel: Yes, we must reflect seriously on this issue. Men must change and recognize the paths traveled by women in the history of humanity.

In addition to giving birth, as we have already mentioned, women's concern for and commitment to life are much more solid and enduring than those of men. In Latin America, we have always known that the paths of liberation cannot be traversed without the presence of women. It is absolutely fundamental to give meaning to existence, and hope to the people. Women have always shown courage and decisiveness; they could offer illuminating lessons in resistance and maturity in the concrete struggles of life to the many men who consider them the "weaker sex."

Gandhi put it this way:

If only women will forget that they belong to the weaker sex, I have no doubt that they can do infinitely more than men against war. Answer for yourselves what your great soldiers and generals would do, if their wives and daughters and mothers refused to countenance their participation in militarism in any shape or form.[11]

In Latin America, many women are forced to rely on themselves or support from other women facing similar difficulties. They must raise and educate their children in very challenging circumstances, and not a few of them must face life and its difficulties on their own. The women's movement has grown over time and consolidated itself through the efforts of such women, and their examples and the testimony of their lives have earned them support and solidarity from broad sectors of society.

Ikeda: I agree that it is impossible to achieve lasting peace without expanding the solidarity of women.

I have engaged in a dialogue with Count Richard Coudenhove-Kalergi (1894–1972), a leading proponent of European unification. He once observed that the will to fight and to kill is an impulse traditionally attributed to the masculine, while the will to have consideration for others and to care for them prevails, above all, in the feminine.[12]

In general, values such as creative coexistence, unity, harmony, and peace are identified as feminine. All of these can only be manifested through our free volition, emerging from within us. In contrast, externally imposed, coercive forces inflicted on other lives, such as opposition, rejection, and war, are usually identified as masculine.

Women suffered horribly from the war and violence of the twentieth century. Nor has the negative heritage resulting from the domination of the masculine principle yet been eradicated. In the twenty-first century, however, such fundamental values for human existence as life, heart, spirit, and family are beginning to be reevaluated and reaffirmed. These are akin to feminine principles.

A shift from competition to harmonious cooperation, from external coercion to inner volition—surely the revival of such feminine principles is the key to redirecting the twenty-first century toward becoming a century of life and peace. A society where women can smile radiantly and act vigorously is a society that as a whole—men included—is blessed with harmony and dynamism, and promises a future illuminated with hope.

The twenty-first century is increasingly in need of the spirit of women, with their compassion for life and their stubborn refusal to countenance violence.

Esquivel: I agree. All projects are enriched and excellent results are obtained when women's resources are successfully deployed. In Uruguay, Paraguay, and Costa Rica, female SERPAJ comrades have developed various educational activities for the defense of human rights. In all our offices they share responsibilities with men on an equal footing, with the same rights.

Through a wide variety of programs, they are working to promote the resolution of conflicts by nonviolent means. They are demonstrating an extremely fundamental value: that women are constructors of peace and understanding among individuals and peoples.

Moving beyond Societies Governed by the Forces of Discrimination and Oppression

Ikeda: That is wonderful.

The great Indian poet Rabindranath Tagore (1861–1941) addressed the issue of what we may hope for from women in terms of our civilization, declaring:

> At the present stage of history civilization is almost exclusively masculine, a civilization of power . . .
>
> Men have been losing their freedom and their humanity in order to fit themselves for vast mechanical organizations. So the next civilization, it is hoped, will be based not merely upon economical and political competition and exploitation but upon worldwide social co-operation; upon spiritual ideals of reciprocity, and not upon economic ideals of efficiency. And then women will have their true place.

But woman can bring her fresh mind and all her power of sympathy to this new task of building up a spiritual civilization, if she will be conscious of her responsibilities.[13]

In other words, in the past civilization of power, human beings have been treated as mere means and have lost their spirituality. In the task of building a new civilization of the spirit, women will play the leading role, says Tagore. We must therefore hope that they will be given a broader stage for activities in all countries and all fields of endeavor.

Esquivel: I agree. Unfortunately, those stages for activity you mention are still nonexistent or very precarious in certain countries.

In some nations, because of religious intolerance, women are forced to live in exclusion as if they were inferior beings, and their social activity is restricted. Nonetheless, in many nations, the presence of women is becoming increasingly important in cultural, scientific, political, and technical circles.

In many countries women have managed to free themselves from a marginalized position, from restriction to the roles of homemaker and child raiser, and to break out of the mold of being considered only a means of reproduction or pleasure.

Beginning in the second half of the nineteenth century, the discriminatory view of women began changing. Women have continued to engage in resistance movements, creating new spaces for their participation in society, fighting for women's rights and equality and the right to exercise their freedom. Through their efforts, they have destroyed the rigid system of the male monopolization of society.

Ikeda: It is certainly true that throughout history women have been oppressed and exploited. Even in the twentieth century, in spite of the great strides of economic development in some nations, many women were forced into extreme poverty.

At the same time, women's rights became a focal point on a global scale and their right to vote and hold elected office gained wide acceptance. The birth of the Convention on the Elimination of All Forms of Discrimination against Women[14] in the last quarter of the twentieth century is symbolic of an irreversible current.

Esquivel: Yes, it is, but progress has been slow, laborious, and in many instances painful. Men have remained unwilling to give women space for action outside the family sphere. The struggle has been unequal because power has remained in the hands of the patriarchy.

Women's victories in overcoming discrimination have depended on social struggles and enormous individual and collective intellectual capacity. After gaining the right to vote and hold elected office, they have pressed on to become active in society, politics, culture, science, and other areas.

The great scientist Marie Curie broke the shackles of her epoch and opened new possibilities for female participation in fields formerly restricted exclusively to men. In doing this, she made a very important contribution to humanity.

Ikeda: There is a statue of Marie Curie at Soka Women's College in Tokyo, which I founded. Her granddaughter, Hélène Langevin-Joliot, a French nuclear physicist, visited the campus and engaged in heartwarming exchanges with students.

As is exemplified by her two Nobel Prizes—in physics (1903) and chemistry (1911)—Marie Curie's achievements as a scientist opened a new era in the history of the intellectual accomplishments of women.

Shining with special nobility among her achievements are her self-sacrificing acts during World War I. Ignoring personal danger, she and her daughter visited the front lines to assist the wounded, treating some of them with cutting-edge X-ray medical technology.

After the war, she actively promoted peace in the League of Nations. "I think," said Curie, "that one can have an interesting and useful life at any age. What is necessary is not to waste it and to be able to say, 'I did what I could.'"[15] "I mostly think of what has to be done and not of what has been done."[16]

Throughout history many women have persevered in striving to turn the path of humanity in the direction of goodness, hope, and peace. In an age plunged into confusion and anxiety by war, violence, oppression, human rights violations, disease, and hunger, it is women who, for the sake of their beloved children and families, have risen up to expand compassion to society as a whole in the effort to build a better tomorrow.

Lady Shrimala and Mother Teresa

Ikeda: Buddhist scriptures and history provide many examples of brilliantly active women.

One of them is Lady Shrimala or Queen Shrimala,[17] who made a vow to Shakyamuni and followed through on it with actions to alleviate the sufferings of others: "When I see living beings who are lonely, imprisoned, ill, and afflicted by various misfortunes and hardships, I will never forsake them, even for a moment, for I must bring them peace. Through my good deeds I will bring them benefits and liberate them from their pain."[18]

"I shall seek to convert the sentient beings with my mind unoccupied with material things, ever unsatisfied, and not retreating."[19]

Esquivel: I remember you telling us of Lady Shrimala when my wife and I met you in Tokyo in 1995. You described her as a woman who pledged herself to protecting human rights.

Her story reminds me of Mother Teresa (1910–97), whom I met on several occasions. As a Catholic nun, she devoted herself to the impoverished, marginalized people on the verge of a despairing, lonely death, such as the so-called untouchables, or *harijan,* of Kolkata (former Calcutta).

When asked about the world situation, Mother Teresa said she had no understanding of the political, economic, or financial problems that occupied politicians. Afflicted by the sufferings of others, the most important thing to her was "putting love into action." I think this exemplifies a path without words.

Ikeda: That is a philosophically very profound statement.

Because their ultimate goal must be the happiness of humanity, I believe that politics and economics must be founded on the religious spirit of love and compassion.

The spirit of compassion symbolized by Lady Shrimala courses through Nichiren Buddhism. Nichiren, who lived during the thirteenth century, a time when the ordinary people suffered bitterly in a series of wars and disasters, composed his treatise "On Establishing the Correct Teaching for the Peace of the Land" as an admonition to the authorities of the Kamakura shogunate.

In it, instead of the typical Chinese character for "land," which is the ideograph for "king" enclosed in a square frame suggesting the ruler's domain, he uses the character with the ideograph for "the people" enclosed in a frame. In other words, he thought of a nation not as its rulers or as a territory but as the ordinary people living there, and his treatise focuses on their happiness and tranquility. This is the equivalent of the contemporary idea of what we call "human security."

"On Establishing the Correct Teaching for the Peace of the Land" articulates the idea that the ordinary people must be the protagonists in changing the world for the better, manifesting their full potential based on the principle of the respect for the dignity of life.

Nichiren promotes a harmonious way of life, urging us to seek peace for all humanity if we wish to ensure our own happiness. He writes: "If you care anything about your personal security, you should first of all pray for order and tranquillity throughout the four quarters of the land, should you not?"[20]

Adopting Nichiren's philosophy of peace and his view of the state as the core of our personal philosophy inevitably leads us to take action for world peace and the happiness of all people. At the same time, it activates us to fight against the devilish nature of authority and all other threats that violate human dignity.

The SGI, in cooperation with UN organizations like the United Nations High Commissioner for Refugees (UNHCR), has produced exhibitions on the theme of human rights and engaged in contribution campaigns for refugees. These efforts are motivated by our beliefs as Buddhists upholding the philosophy of respect for the dignity of life.

The Declaration of Women's Rights in the Lotus Sutra

Esquivel: I know that since its foundation as a great lay organization based on the teachings of Nichiren, the Soka Gakkai has consistently worked for the peace and happiness of humanity, but I would like to know what view Shakyamuni had of women.

Ikeda: Extreme discrimination against women prevailed in Indian society of Shakyamuni's time. Numerous passages in the Brahmanic scriptures speak contemptuously and insultingly of women. But Shakyamuni directed his teachings equally to men and women, affirming their equality in religious matters and accepting the ordination of women within the Buddhist order. Historically speaking, this was truly remarkable.

After his death, however, the Buddhist order succumbed to the discriminatory views of the times and began to adopt a male-centric stance, adopting the doctrine of the five obstacles or five hindrances to a woman's attainments, which stated that a woman could not become a Brahmā, a Shakra, a devil king, a wheel-turning king, or a Buddha. In addition, women were labeled emissaries of hell and declared to lack the "seed" (the potential) to become Buddhas. In other words, women were declared eternally ineligible to attain enlightenment.

In that context, the Lotus Sutra's teaching of the attainment of Buddhahood by women carried on Shakyamuni's teaching of the equality of the sexes. In the "Devadatta" chapter of the Lotus Sutra, the eight-year-old dragon king's daughter attains enlightenment.

In this chapter, Shakyamuni's disciple Shariputra expresses his disbelief in the possibility that women, subject to the five hindrances, can attain enlightenment. The dragon king's daughter declares in response: "Employ your supernatural powers and watch me attain buddhahood."[21]

This revolutionary statement utterly rejecting the prevailing discrimination against women was a great human rights declaration.

Esquivel: Shakyamuni's attitude toward women must have been highly revolutionary for the India of his time.

What attitudes toward women characterized the Japan of Nichiren's day?

Ikeda: Medieval Japan was a patriarchal society, and Japanese Buddhism, which had lost the spirit of Shakyamuni, also held discriminatory attitudes toward women. It was a time when women were severely discriminated against in every respect. Against that background, Nichiren insisted that in terms of religious practice and capability for enlightenment men and women are completely equal.

The following words clearly reflect his view of women: "Only in the Lotus Sutra do we read that a woman who embraces this sutra not only excels all other women, but also surpasses all men."[22]

"There should be no discrimination among those who propagate the five characters of Myoho-renge-kyo in the Latter Day of the Law, be they men or women."[23]

"Are not all practitioners of the Lotus Sutra, both men and women, World-Honored Ones [Buddhas]?"[24]

Nichiren wrote many letters of encouragement to women, whom he addressed with titles of great respect he rarely employed when writing to men. He had supreme respect for women.

Esquivel: If I understand correctly, then, he made no distinction between laity and clergy or between men and women, and offered the highest praise and encouragement to his female followers.

Ikeda: That's correct. As I noted earlier, Shakyamuni stated: "Not by birth does one become an outcaste, not by birth does one become a brahman. By [one's] action one becomes an outcaste, by [one's] action one becomes a brahman."[25]

Neither Shakyamuni nor Nichiren ever discriminated among people on the basis of sex or class, family origin, or membership in the laity or the clergy. For them, nobility or baseness depend solely on the individual's deeds and mental attitudes. The important thing is not gender but whether a person is able to bring his or her limitless possibilities to full flower and find happiness. This, I believe, is the spirit of both Shakyamuni and Nichiren.

Instead of being obsessed by gender differences, we must strive to perfect and fulfill ourselves.

Esquivel: Your explanation has made the Buddhist view of women clear to me. And this in turn explains why the Soka Gakkai, based on the philosophy of Shakyamuni and Nichiren, respects and places great significance on women.

President Makiguchi's Emphasis on Educating Women

Ikeda: I am sure your recognition of our stance on this matter will serve as a great source of encouragement for the future efforts of the women of the SGI. In our movement for peace, we are engaged in a constant effort to adapt the teachings of Buddhism to contemporary society and make them relevant and effective. Tsunesaburo Makiguchi, first president of the Soka Gakkai, held the highest expectations for women, asserting that "mothers are the original educators and the ones who will build the ideal future society"[26] and calling for a great awakening of maternal instinct.

As an educator, President Makiguchi regarded the education of women as extremely important.

In 1904, at the height of the Russo-Japanese War (1904–05), he was a teacher at Toa Girl's School in Tokyo and founded and managed the Japan Women's Higher Education Association. The association offered correspondence courses for young women who had graduated from elementary school (the equivalent of modern junior high school), waiving entrance fees and offering special tuition rates for families of soldiers at the front. It also had a system for recognizing model students. For girls unable to pay the association's fees, Mr. Makiguchi initiated a free institute of the applied arts.

His commitment to encouraging and reaching out to young women is exemplified by the publication in 1907 of *Nihon no Shojo* (The Japanese Girl) by the National Japanese Girls' Association, which he also managed. It was the second-oldest periodical of its kind in the country at the time. His activities for women's education were based on his commitment to making education available to all.

Esquivel: That's most impressive.

Taking such action in the name of women's education at the beginning of the twentieth century was indeed highly innovative.

Education is the basis of all society. It not only imparts knowledge but also fosters awareness. It gives women the creative vitality and emotional strength to maintain inner and outer equilibrium in the face of the damaging impacts of the conflict and trauma they encounter in society.

Ikeda: Precisely.

In *Daikatei* (The Great Family), a correspondence learning publication for girls which was sent monthly to members of the Japan Women's Higher Education Association, Mr. Makiguchi published a speech in which he said:

Are there people in the world today who don't feel the need for women's education? The era of suppressing the love of learning and claiming that learning is useless and dangerous for women has passed . . .

I want to use education to keep women from falling into poverty.

Providing jobs for women is superior to simply giving them money, and providing them the ability to discover on their own ways to make their living and overcome difficulties is superior to providing jobs.[27]

Second Soka Gakkai president Josei Toda, also an educator, inherited Mr. Makiguchi's convictions and engaged in efforts for correspondence-course education. As third Soka Gakkai president, I founded the Soka Women's College and have established correspondence-education courses in Soka University to realize Mr. Makiguchi's and Mr. Toda's ideals.

In addition, the Kansai Soka Junior and Senior High Schools, with their mottoes of common sense, good health, and hope, started originally as the Soka Girls' Junior and Senior High Schools in Kansai. At the first entrance ceremony for the school I presented the students with the important principle I mentioned previously of not building one's own happiness on the misfortune of others.

Esquivel: So the challenge of providing education for women has been inherited and carried on by the three successive presidents of the Soka Gakkai.

The high expectations Mr. Makiguchi had for women and his call for "a great awakening of maternal instinct" illuminates the path that we should press forward on now, in the twenty-first century.

The Soka Gakkai has pursued a path leading to liberty and peace. The pioneering individuals who founded it have followed the path of peace and solidarity with the intention of radically transforming spiritual values in every aspect of life.

Women Civilizing Humanity through the Power of Dialogue

Esquivel: Many of us hoped that with the fall of the Berlin Wall (in 1989) and the end of the Cold War the world had begun moving toward peace. We thought that from then on humanity would focus all its efforts on the elimination of hunger and poverty and concentrate on protecting the global environment.

But reality turned out to be much more complicated. Ethnic conflicts and terrorism continue unabated and the global problems confronting humanity, such as war, famine, poverty, and environmental destruction, assumed still more alarming forms.

The balance between humankind and nature has been lost, and the world has become engulfed in violence and uncertainty. At the same time, high illiteracy rates and insufficient resources to ensure human health and development have become pressing threats.

Ikeda: True. In the hope of focusing on such problems and discovering hints for resolving them, for some years I have been issuing annual peace proposals. In addition, prior to the September 2006 meeting of the United Nations General Assembly, I published a proposal entitled "Fulfilling the Mission: Empowering the UN to Live Up to the World's Expectations."

In it, I wrote that in spite of the various problems and criticisms of the United Nations, as long as there are people in the world threatened by famine, poverty, and environmental pollution, the only path to resolving those issues is fortifying and invigorating the UN, to which most of the world's nations belong and which continues its activities around the globe to support humanity.

In the all-important area of education, in spite of a moderate increase in children attending primary school all over the world, there are still 785 million illiterate adults worldwide according to UNESCO estimates.[28] Of this number, two-thirds are women. More than a hundred million children are said to be deprived of the chance to attend school.

The expansion of basic education and equal educational opportunities are urgent issues. UNESCO plays a central part in conducting the campaign Education for All (EFA), and in connection with this goal, in 2003 the United Nations started its UN Literacy Decade.

Esquivel: Certainly the work of international organizations such as the UN has borne fruit. Nonetheless, many different kinds of walls dividing humanity persist; for example, the wall between the rich and the poor, the wall between Israel and Palestine, the wall dividing North and South Korea, and the wall between the United States and Mexico. These walls deepen rifts among peoples by intensifying hatred and provoking acts of retaliation.

Without doubt, however, the most difficult walls to raze are the walls within our own hearts erected by intolerance, failure to engage in dialogue, and the lust for power and conquest. Such walls can be torn down only by means of a daily process of one-to-one dialogue and active engagement in social and cultural interactions.

Ikeda: I agree. In speaking with Betty Williams, we discussed ways humanity can break the vicious circle of hatred and vengeance. She said, "For me, and the only way I can work, is to remain true to one's beliefs and love one's opponents into submission. This is by no means an easy thing to do."

Candid, open, one-to-one dialogue is the only way to eliminate the walls of intolerance and discrimination dwelling in people's hearts. I believe that the only prospect for establishing lasting peace is steady, persistent dialogue to develop people's inherent good qualities, such traits as compassion and courage, and thus build a network of goodness.

Dialogue is our weapon for peace. And perhaps it can be said that women are better at dialogue than men.

Great thinkers of the past who have stressed the importance of dialogue have called attention to women's special capacity for dialogue. One of them, Ralph Waldo Emerson (1803–82) stressed that for dialogue to search deepest, rise highest, and produce the greatest benefit, it must be between two individuals. You have made the same point, Dr. Esquivel.

Emerson also observed: "Women are, by this [wise, cultivated, genial conversation] and their social influence, the civilizers of mankind. What is civilization? I answer, the power of good women."[29] Surely the power of women will initiate and guide the age of dialogue.

Esquivel: I agree.

History is nourished by a rich flow of the experiences and contributions of many women who worked for the people's liberation. Particularly in the twentieth century, which was marked by violence, wars, and armed conflicts that inflicted profound damage on human life and spirit, this flow acted as a model to facilitate the constant evolution of humanity.

Ikeda: SGI women members have ceaselessly struggled to build peace with a resilient spirit undaunted by violence and terrorism. The journalist Mariane Pearl is one of them.

Her husband Daniel Pearl, a correspondent for the *Wall Street Journal,* was abducted and killed by an armed group in January 2002, while on assignment in Pakistan. The terrorists behind the killing shocked people all over the world by posting the murder on the Internet.

It is hard even to imagine the depth and scope of his wife's sorrow. She was pregnant with their son at the time. But she refused to be defeated. She began writing a book, *A Mighty Heart: The Brave Life and Death of My Husband Danny Pearl* (2003), in which, describing that event, she declared that if she allowed her suffering to get the better of her, it would cost her soul. Hating the criminals would only satisfy their wish to plunge her husband and her into fear and submission and make them powerless, which was just what the terrorists wanted. She said she intended to win this battle to overcome hatred for the sake of the happiness of her son, who had never seen his father's face.[30]

Her memoir aroused great public response and in 2003 received the French Prix Verité for outstanding factual reporting. In the message of condolence I sent to services marking the first anniversary of the tragedy, I said that the global sorrow caused by Daniel Pearl's death has created a vast network of human solidarity, and not even the most hate-filled can destroy this force for good.

The Struggle to Rouse Humanity's Conscience

Esquivel: I completely agree with your way of thinking. Women are becoming protagonists of social change and engaging in an effort to forge a new conscience for humanity.

Recently I have been having encounters and interchanges of ideas with teachers and other professionals in the fields of education, psychology, and the law as well as with social workers, instructors at various levels, and students. Most of these people are women of extraordinary dynamic powers striving to create interdisciplinary networks in various fields. I feel that their silent revolution of the conscience will generate new social paradigms.

Women are assuming new roles and places for action in their societies. In Argentina and throughout the Latin American continent mighty women's movements have arisen in defense of human rights, like the ones I have already mentioned: the Mothers and Grandmothers of the Plaza de Mayo, the families of the imprisoned and disappeared, and similar expressions of solidarity among actresses, singers, writers, musicians, and many other female intellectuals.

Ikeda: The people you mention are noble pioneers in the creation of the century of women. In our SGI movement for peace, culture, and education too, women display wonderful strengths and are playing leading roles in various activities.

For example, the Soka Gakkai Women's Peace Committee is engaged in such publishing projects as the twenty-volume series entitled *With Hopes for Peace* and sponsoring a variety of exhibitions to raise public awareness, including "Women and the Pacific War," "Mothers, Children, and War," "Our Global Family," "Women and the Culture of Peace," and "Children and the Culture of Peace."

They are also involved in sponsoring lectures, mass meetings on important topics, and collecting petition signatures to communicate the message of peace.

Esquivel: I am immensely happy to know that the SGI is making such efforts in the name of peace and that its women are dedicated protagonists of value creation in expanding the importance of understanding the problems confronting humanity. Women acting as the protagonists striving for the realization of peace gives great hope for our times.

And the times are changing. We are moving from individualism toward a network of solidarity and shared struggle and hope for the people.

We must strive for freedom, not singly, but all together.

Ikeda: That is indeed the principle for the liberation of the people.

Esquivel: When women break their silence and rise up conscientiously, the world cannot fail but to change for the better.

In this connection, I am reminded of the saying, "The barking of dogs signals that we are riding forth."

The eruption of women into the life of the twenty-first century promises to bring many surprises signifying hope for the arrival of a new dawn.

Ikeda: You quoted the same saying before leaving Japan at the time of our first meeting in 1995. On that occasion, you said, "When someone I have great faith in is attacked, insulted, and persecuted, I will say nothing to him. But when that person ceases to be criticized, then I will express dissatisfaction—because that means he has given up the fight."

I was deeply impressed. This is the kind of sentiment we can expect to hear from a person like you who has overcome hardship time and time again.

The waves stirred by a ship in full sail are proof of forward motion. Your words are a tremendous encouragement to those of us who have struggled against groundless demagoguery and envious criticism.

Esquivel: I am very happy that you still remember my words.

I am aware of the calumny and baseless lies the three successive presidents of the Soka Gakkai have endured.

Ikeda: I have composed a poem expressing my thoughts concerning women as the protagonists of the century of life:

With the new sun
a new century of women has come.
The century of women
is the victory of a life
in which women gain
happiness
and the right to peace.
It is a victory of their movement,
the victory of their activities,
the victory of their advance,
the victory of survival,
the victory of their families.
. . . .
Cheers to the strong women
soaring without limits
into the new century!

Peace is not something removed from our daily existence. The movement of SGI women aiming to build a culture of peace is based on their steadfast, persevering efforts for dialogue in their families and communities.

I am certain that the struggle waged by these determined women and mothers will open the door of hope for the century of human rights.

FIVE

Youth—The Key to Building a Culture of Peace

Nuclear Weapons Are an Absolute Evil— Thoughts on Hiroshima

Ikeda: Many years have passed since I first met you and your wife in Tokyo in 1995. Forming a friendship with a great peace and human rights leader like you over the years spanning the last century and into the present one is one of the proudest experiences of my life.

Allow me to thank you sincerely for the heartfelt message of congratulations you sent on the occasion of my eightieth birthday.

Esquivel: I would like to take this opportunity to repeat my sincere wishes for your peace and well-being and extend my heartfelt felicitations. I have the highest admiration and respect for your life of eighty years, dedicated to sharing the struggle and hopes for building a more just and fraternal world for all humanity.

Please accept greetings from my wife, Amanda, and my sons, as well as from the entire SERPAJ in Latin America.

Ikeda: Thank you, and please extend my best wishes to your fondly remembered, intelligent wife, to your whole family, and to the members of all the branches of your highly respected organization.

Though as a youth I was in such frail health that my doctor predicted I would be lucky to see the age of thirty, I have now reached a healthy eighty and am resolved that my remaining years shall be devoted to the important task of putting the finishing touches on my life.

I have expressed that resolution as follows: "At eighty, opening the future with the youth. At eighty, opening the way for an age of peace together with thinking people around the world."[1] This is a reflection of my present state of mind. This is why I consider it a real honor to conduct a dialogue for building a peaceful century with you, who have consistently risked your very life to protect the human rights and dignity of the people.

Esquivel: Let us do just that!

In this age of dialogue, the clarity of your thinking, your concern for the life of our societies, for spirituality, and the welfare of the people, and, in particular, your concern for the future of young people are plainly evident.

Along the road you have traveled, there are many courageous women, who have lived through struggles and achievements, sharing the collective memory of the people, their values and identity. Under your leadership, the Soka Gakkai is contributing to fostering critical awareness among the people by promoting the values of education, as a practice of freedom and peace. In your long and productive life, you have applied your experience and wisdom to the task of strengthening values and knowledge.

Ikeda: Once again, I fear you praise me too generously.

As you suggest, the cultivation of the people's critical awareness, in particular their ability to distinguish between right and wrong, good and evil, will determine the future, human happiness, and peace.

In our society that distinction is sometimes obscured, but harming, debasing, and taking life, which is sacred, are always evil and wrong, and protecting and nurturing life are always right and good. That much is certain.

And this is why I have said that nuclear weapons are an absolute evil.

I have consistently urged and taken action to see that Hiroshima and Nagasaki, the targets of atomic weapons, are etched in human history as the eternal starting point of the movement to renounce war completely.

Esquivel: I agree entirely. Hiroshima is unforgettably burned into my mind and heart.

Ikeda: As a human rights activist and proponent of nonviolence, I am certain that you unconditionally reject nuclear weapons. You have called Hiroshima a victim to the ultimate violence.

In the autumn of 1988, you and your wife traveled to Hiroshima for the first time, visiting the Hiroshima Peace Memorial Museum and the Cenotaph for Atomic-bomb Victims and listening to the stories related by the survivors of the bombing. Expressing your reaction, you said that you thought you were aware of the horrors of the atomic bombings, but now having seen them with your own eyes, you realized it was a tragedy on a scale exceeding all imagining. The experience, you said, inspired you to persevere with even greater zeal in your work for peace.

In an act of great goodwill, you immediately created a bronze sculpture expressing the destruction of property and human life and presented it to the city of Hiroshima the following year when you visited Japan.

I believe you have said that the statue represents the hope that humanity, with its gaze set on the horizon of the twenty-first century, would be able to recover from the tremendous loss represented by the bombing of Hiroshima. The citizens of Hiroshima, who have long struggled in the name of peace, were deeply touched by your gift.

What other impressions did your visit to Hiroshima make on you?

Esquivel: I can still see the looks on the faces of some girls in photographs I viewed in the museum—the girls who survived the bombing. Many years have passed and they have matured and grown old, but something has marked them forever, something they cannot forget, something we must not forget. That terrible moment is forever engraved in their expressions.

They are the witnesses for the people of Japan and the entire world to that moment when the human race lost its breath and the heart of the world stopped. When Robert A. Lewis (1917–83), the co-pilot of the bomber that dropped the bomb, witnessed the result of his destructive work, he cried out in horror: "My God, what have we done?"

Whenever I see the chiefs of state of either great powers or developing countries bent on using nuclear arms as a way of fortifying their power, Hiroshima comes to mind immediately.

Hiroshima has left a mark on humanity. Nuclear armaments clearly reveal what the power of the science we have created can lead to and the costs of its consequences and risks for present and future generations of the world.

Ikeda: Humanity must never repeat that tragedy.

I have many friends who were exposed to the bombings of Hiroshima and Nagasaki and have courageously shared their experiences with the world.

Our organization, with our young people, especially those of both cities, taking the lead, has conducted an extensive program of interviews and tape recordings documenting the experiences of victims, as well as sponsoring a series of antiwar publications, to ensure that each of their stories is preserved for posterity. In addition, we have sponsored exhibitions, lectures, and questionnaires on peace and the dignity of life, driving our message home in our communities and around the world.

On your visit to the Hiroshima Peace Memorial Museum in 1995, you saw the stone in which the outline of a victim of the bombing remains dark against a background bleached by radiation. You called that stone "The Shadow of Humanity." On the same occasion, you called for an immediate cessation of all nuclear testing, speaking out courageously and rightly as an advocate for the feelings of all the victims.

I am reminded of the remarks of Richard von Weizsäcker, first president of united Germany, upon his visit to Hiroshima. He said that the misery caused by the inhuman explosion was indescribable and that to his knowledge no other place on Earth more clearly demonstrated to all who saw it the need and the reason for eliminating those inhuman weapons. He said that no city could so strongly incite the desire for peace as Hiroshima. He also said that the vitality of Hiroshima, its will to live, its economic drive, its culture, and its natural beauty inspire hope for the future.[2]

I have always argued that all world leaders, especially those of nations possessing nuclear weapons, should go to Hiroshima and Nagasaki to see for themselves how cruel nuclear weapons are and how horrific is the disaster they wreak.

A Leadership Revolution for the Sake of Peace

Esquivel: I agree completely.

Those in power refuse to understand that nuclear armaments, rather than guaranteeing the security of the nations that possess them, only create greater insecurity and imperil the lives of their own people and of all humanity.

I realize that advances in technical and scientific knowledge are important to many countries, and that whether nuclear energy is used for developmental or destructive aims is a political decision of governments.

A reading of the policies of today's great powers and the world situation shows that unfortunately those in power have no desire to register or take into account the clear demands of their peoples. Certain political leaders demonstrate an insane lust for economic, political, and military power. Their memories of the tragedies of human history are vague and blurred. As a result, they ignore the people's suffering and unleash wars and invasions. Blinded by power, they inflict even further death and destruction on the people.

Ikeda: As was true in the militaristic Japan of the past, the devilish nature of authority wreaks untold misery on the ordinary people.

The more power a person exercises, the more arrogant he or she becomes, disregarding the dignity of other people's lives and inflicting immeasurable pain and misery. Consequently, in this nuclear age of horrifyingly murderous weapons, a revolution in the nature of leaders is absolutely essential to prevent the recurrence of such a tragedy.

Esquivel: I am reminded in this context of Einstein. In November 1945, he contributed a letter to an American magazine in which he offered an historic message:

> The release of atomic energy has not created a new problem. It has merely made more urgent the necessity of solving an existing one ... As long as there are sovereign nations possessing great power, war is inevitable. That is not an attempt to say when it will come, but only that it is sure to come. That was true before the atomic bomb was made. What has been changed is the destructiveness of war.[3]

Later in the letter he said: "I do not consider myself the father of the release of atomic energy. My part in it was quite indirect. I did not, in fact, foresee that it would be released in my time."[4] He added: "Since I do not foresee that atomic energy is to be a great boon for a long time, I have to say that for the present it is a menace."[5]

Many years have passed since Einstein composed this letter, and the menace he referred to still exists. Now, however, it is not only the great powers who possess nuclear armaments. Other nations have managed to acquire the technology. Yet in spite of this, the thinking and attitudes of leaders remain unchanged.

Ikeda: Precisely. A revolution of leadership is necessary. And the people must grow in wisdom and strength in order to bring about that revolution.

What are your thoughts about the present situation with regard to nuclear weapons?

Esquivel: The five great powers who are permanent members of the United Nations Security Council have at their disposal huge nuclear arsenals capable of destroying every living thing on Earth. The powers that rule our world today are dashing at breakneck speed toward military might and nuclear armament. I doubt that the end of the Cold War terminated the competition between the United States and Russia.

Besides, other nations that have developed technology and possess atomic weapons also want to become members of the nuclear "club of death." Israel is one of them but, as an ally of the United States, little is said about its nuclear arsenal. From the Israel–Palestine perspective, coupled with the regional instability in Iran, the situation in the Middle East grows worse.

The great powers have no intention of beginning real disarmament. They intend to be the sole possessors of the arms of mass destruction that permit them to control and subjugate the rest of the world. As long as they are unprepared to disarm, the arms race will continue and go on imperiling global peace.

In each country, hate, intolerance, and rivalry stimulate development of the destructive power of nuclear arms with the idea that greater military power and the possession of hypocritically named "weapons of deterrence" result in greater influence.

Ikeda: The arms race you speak of with such dismay is the pinnacle of the cycle of evil that human beings are fated to repeat over and over, a manifestation of what the Buddhist philosophy of the nature of life describes as the world of *asuras*.

This is a life state of extreme selfishness, in which one is compelled to constantly compare oneself to and subjugate others. This evil impulse to dominate allows no room for respect for other people; it doesn't hesitate to destroy others, who are regarded only as means for the satisfaction of one's own selfish ego.

Buddhism describes human life states in terms of ten categories, or the Ten Worlds. Starting at the lowest and moving upward, they are the worlds of hell, hungry spirits, animals, *asuras*, human beings, heavenly beings, voice-hearers, cause-awakened ones, bodhisattvas, and Buddhas.

The majority of human beings spend their time moving through the so-called six paths—the six lower life states from hell to heavenly beings. The life state of *asuras*, one of those six, always has a high likelihood of manifesting itself. In fact, it is extremely characteristic of human society as a whole.

But collisions between beings in the life state of *asuras* can only result in endless conflict and destruction. In the final analysis, the insatiable arms race spells defeat for humanity itself.

Esquivel: Yes, that is its logical conclusion. But how can the human race begin real disarmament? Many are asking the following questions:

Have we forgotten the suffering of humanity?

Have we forgotten what happened during World War II?

Have we become oblivious to Hiroshima and Nagasaki, the Holocaust, the millions of lost lives, the horror, the deaths, and the consequences that persist still today in the lives and awareness of humanity?

In the face of the situation in which human beings now live we must ask ourselves: What can each of us do? What should we do? What can our leaders do?

Expanding the Global Nuclear-free Zone

Ikeda: I completely share your questions and your impassioned call to all of us. And I firmly believe that, no matter how difficult, any situation human beings have created can be rectified by human beings.

One concrete step we can take to eliminate nuclear weapons is to clearly establish their illegality on a global level. We need to build a consensus in international society to affirm the illegality of nuclear armaments.

One promising noteworthy trend in this regard is the expansion of nuclear-free zones.

In 1967, Latin America set the pattern by drawing up the first-ever treaty establishing a non-nuclear zone where all testing, use, production, deployment, and acquisition of nuclear weapons are forbidden. It is a model for a nuclear-free world. As is well known, your own homeland, Argentina, declared its abandonment of nuclear weapons development plans at an early stage.

Esquivel: Quite so. In 1967, the nations of Latin America concluded the Treaty of Tlatelolco on nonproliferation of nuclear arms.

Later, it was expanded to include the nations of the Caribbean region, and its title was altered accordingly to the Treaty for the Prohibition of Nuclear Weapons in Latin America and the Caribbean.

It has been ratified by the thirty-three nations making up the region. All in all, these steps seem encouraging.

Ikeda: They do indeed. And nuclear-free zones are expanding on a global scale.

In 1959, with the adoption of the Antarctic Treaty System, all nuclear explosions and the disposal of nuclear wastes were forbidden south of 60 degrees south latitude. Since then, nuclear-free zones have been expanded to include Latin America and the Caribbean region, as well as the South Pacific, Southeast Asia, Africa, and Central Asia.

At present, establishment of a non-nuclear zone encompassing the entire southern hemisphere is underway, and more than one hundred countries have signed non-nuclear-zone treaties.

As I mentioned in my Peace Proposal for 2008,[6] it is now urgently necessary to develop a similar non-nuclear zone in the Arctic.

We must take the success of the establishment of a non-nuclear zone in the southern hemisphere and now, increasingly, in Asia, and use it as a basis for establishing a consensus for outlawing nuclear weapons as the norm for all humanity. That is my cherished wish.

In the opaque conditions that have followed the conclusion of the Cold War, the danger of proliferation as a result of traffic in nuclear materials and technologies increases. In these circumstances the decision by the Latin American nations, including Argentina, to go non-nuclear was a truly wise and historic development.

Esquivel: That is so, and in terms of Asia, the whole world expects Japan, as the victim of nuclear attacks, to assume a leadership role in the elimination of these weapons.

Making the Spirit of the Antinuclear Declaration a Reality

Ikeda: Indeed. Contributing to the eradication of nuclear weapons and to building peace is Japan's mission.

As his primary parting instruction to young people, in September 1957, the year before his death, Josei Toda denounced nuclear weapons as an absolute evil.

His historic declaration reads in part:

We, the citizens of the world, have an inviolable right to live. Anyone who jeopardizes that right is a devil incarnate, a

fiend, a monster . . . Even if a country should conquer the
world through the use of nuclear weapons, the conquerors
must be viewed as devils, as evil incarnate. I believe that it is
the mission of every member of the youth division in Japan
to disseminate this idea throughout the globe.[7]

Mr. Toda saw the devilish desire to ruthlessly destroy others' lives
as the origin and essential character of nuclear weapons, and for that
reason, he stressed that along with disarmament, we need a movement
promoting human revolution to defeat the devilish nature that
resides in the depths of human beings. Unless human beings
themselves changed and ended the vicious cycle of hatred and fear,
disarmament remained a pipe dream and the situation was bound to
grow even worse, making lasting peace an impossibility.

Joseph Rotblat, another Nobel Peace Prize laureate, was intensely
sympathetic with the ideas expressed in Mr. Toda's declaration
against nuclear weapons. Dr. Rotblat was a physicist and president
of the Pugwash Conferences on Science and World Affairs, a group
of scientists seeking the abolition of nuclear weapons.

My mentor Josei Toda delivered his declaration in 1957. In that
same year, Dr. Rotblat established the Pugwash Conferences. He felt
a profound resonance between his efforts and the spirit of Toda's
declaration, both committed to creating a world free of war and
nuclear weapons.

Dr. Rotblat stated that evil cannot be conquered with evil and
that the threat of war should not be used as a way to avert war. He
also said that possessing nuclear arms, even for preemptive purposes,
is immoral—though unfortunately, as he observed, that has become
the norm for all nuclear nations.[8]

I think his attitude agrees with your own concerns.

In any case, the road to peace must give first preeminence to the
security and happiness of the people. The time has come for world
leaders to be deeply aware of this, pool their wisdom, and act to
make it a reality.

Esquivel: I think so, too. The people must always be the main concern.

Director General of the International Atomic Energy Agency (IAEA) Mohamed ElBaradei makes an important point, saying that we need to work to establish a system to guarantee peace and security for all. It must, he added, be a system that is people-centered, rather than relying on nuclear weapons or military power. Without a system that ensures everyone's security, he concluded, we cannot have peace.[9]

Security must be based on the life and development of peoples, not their exploitation.

I believe that the possibility for averting confrontations among nations in a region, such as Latin America, is to be found in the unity of people, in achieving consensus, and in encouraging cooperation and solidarity.

Ikeda: I concur entirely.

When I met him in November 2006, in Tokyo, Director General ElBaradei said that our rights as people—our human rights—must take priority over the sovereignty of the state.

We can achieve peace, he said, if we apprehend our unity as human beings, transcending differences of race, ethnic group, religion, and skin color. The realization of how much we share as human beings, he said, can bring about peace. He also suggested that an appreciation of our shared values will put an end to fighting and war because our differences will be recognized as minor matters having nothing to do with human values.[10]

That is why a peace movement promoting a recognition of our shared human values to the peoples of the world is indispensable.

Taking Mr. Toda's antinuclear declaration as our starting point, we of the SGI have long been advancing a movement for peace, by the people and for the people.

For example, in 1974, our youth division members of the Soka Gakkai in Japan collected ten million signatures for a petition to ban atomic and hydrogen bombs. In recognition of their passion, I went to New York to present a bound copy of the signatures personally to Kurt Waldheim (1918–2007), then Secretary-General of the United Nations.

Beginning in the 1980s, we have organized a series of exhibitions including "Nuclear Arms: Threat to Our World," sponsored jointly with the cities of Hiroshima and Nagasaki and the United Nations Department of Public Information, and another exhibition, "Nuclear Arms: Threat to Humanity." These exhibitions have been shown in thirty-nine cities in twenty-four countries, including the Soviet Union and China, and have been visited by more than 1.7 million people.

In 2007, to commemorate the fiftieth anniversary of Mr. Toda's declaration, we initiated a traveling international exhibition called "From a Culture of Violence to a Culture of Peace: Transforming the Human Spirit." The exhibition was conceived as a concrete manifestation of the United Nations' call for popular efforts to raise consciousness about disarmament and nonproliferation.

While striving to arouse public awareness about the elimination of nuclear arms and disarmament, we are also committed to creating a rising tide of change from the present culture of war to a culture of peace.

Violence Is Just Another Form of Self-righteousness

Esquivel: The formation of a culture of peace must be a sustained effort. All actions, in every field and area, must be directed to the culture of peace.

In speaking of peace, in addition to nuclear weapons we must also address such recent events as terrorist attacks and the many different conflicts taking place across the globe. The horrific terrorist attacks on New York and Washington, DC of September 11, 2001, shook the world.

Some see these actions as exemplifying the logic of cause and effect, action and response—attack and counterattack, aggressors and assaulted, victims and victimizers. But I think that they are actually extreme manifestations of a single factor. They are the fruit of irrationality. Somewhere along the way, reason has been lost and irrationality has taken its place.

Some who are struggling with the contradictions in our world and battling against power and domination come to the conclusion that radical change can only be effected by direct violence in such forms as terrorism or genocide. They also believe they are in sole possession of the truth and seek to impose that truth on others.

Violence and self-righteousness are two sides of the same coin. Perpetrators of terrorism are convinced of the truth of their ideological, religious, or political beliefs and construct high walls of intolerance to exclude others. Filled with hate and disturbed in spirit, they listen only to their own words and justify the use of violence with their self-fulfilling arguments.

Firmly attached to their own ideologies and worldviews, they are prepared to adopt any means to achieve their aims. When they have reached that point, other people become an abstraction to them, and they may even deny the reality and existence of all other peoples or religions.

Ikeda: When we can no longer perceive others as human beings, we fall into the fearsome pitfall of straying from the path of humanity. We succumb to the madness of losing what it is that makes us human. Violence, whatever the reason, is the abandonment of our humanity, the demise of humanity.

I joined spiritual leaders from many different areas in contributing an essay, entitled "The Evil over which We Must Triumph," to the book *From the Ashes: A Spiritual Response to the Attack on America*, published shortly after 9/11.

Buddhism is a philosophy of respect for life. Terrorism, which tramples on life, is an absolute evil, no matter what great cause or ideology it is carried out in the name of.

To break the cycle of evil that produced the violence and war of the twentieth century, we must continuously strive to develop the good inherent in human life. Nurturing the good elements of nonviolence, compassion, trust, wisdom, courage, and integrity is the foundation for peace, vanquishing the devilish nature that seeks to harm life.

In this connection, I must recall Linus Pauling (1901–94), the father of modern chemistry, with whom you, too, were on friendly terms. Already ninety-one years old, Dr. Pauling was good enough to travel all the way from San Francisco to attend a lecture entitled "Radicalism Reconsidered: In Search of New Principles of Integration," which I delivered at Claremont McKenna College in 1993. In commenting on my speech, he touched on the Buddhist philosophy of the Ten Worlds.

He said he was particularly impressed by the description of the ninth world, the world of the bodhisattva, a life state of compassion in which one seeks to save all people from suffering. The human race, he observed, would do well to embrace that spirit. If we ask what it is we must do as human beings, he said, he thought it is to strive to attain this realm of human existence, the bodhisattva state, and act accordingly.

To achieve peace it is important to expend efforts in various areas, from government and law to economics, but such efforts alone are insufficient. In order for them to bear fruit, those engaged in the efforts must have great inner strength. They must be motivated to find their own happiness in working for the happiness of others. They must have the inner self-discipline to avoid building their own happiness on the misfortune of others.

That, I believe, is what Dr. Pauling meant when he said we must embrace the spirit of the world of the bodhisattva.

Esquivel: I am happy that you mention Dr. Pauling, a great friend with whom I shared many activities—among them the voyage of the Peace Ship. Departing from Sweden and Norway, the ship took us to the port of Corinto, in Nicaragua. It was a journey to bring support and solidarity to the Nicaraguan people, victims of the war in Central America.

We carried medicines, fertilizers, machinery, and school materials for the people on the boat, but our most basic cargo was solidarity and friendship. Labor unions, the Lutheran Church, and the government of Norway collaborated in the mission, as did another close friend of both of us, George Wald (1906–97), Nobel laureate in Physiology or Medicine.

Ikeda: A ship bearing solidarity and friendship—what a truly wonderful page in history.

Dr. Pauling was a great scientist who devoted his life to peace. His life was that of a bodhisattva, striving for the welfare of those who were suffering. I am sure that his friendship with you will inspire people of future generations and continue to shine with undying brilliance.

Prioritizing Human Security

Esquivel: On September 11, 2001, the day of the terrorist attacks, another piece of shattering information went unnoted by the major information media.

The United Nations Food and Agriculture Organization announced that on that day, and on every other day of the year, throughout the world, 35,615 children died of hunger.

No television channel covered this item. Many national governments and religious organizations said not a word about this terrible genocide by starvation, this "silent bomb" more murderous than war.

Ikeda: You point out a very important fact. You spoke of this "silent bomb" earlier—the extreme poverty and hunger that are the background for modern terrorist attacks, conflict, and war. In other words, one of the causes of direct violence is structural violence, in the forms of exploitation, prejudice, discrimination, poverty, hunger, and disease.

It was in fact the Bengal famine of 1943, which claimed three million victims, that motivated my friend and the former president of the Pugwash Conferences M. S. Swaminathan to study agriculture, tackle the problem of hunger, and bring relief to countless individuals.

Noting the Roman philosopher Seneca's observation that morality and religion are of no interest to the starving, Dr. Swaminathan insists that peace cannot spread when people are ruled by hunger. He stresses that the environmental, economic, physical, and social conditions that provide people with a balanced, nutritious diet and clean drinking water should be the fundamental human rights guaranteed to all people.[11]

I agree with him. We must make promoting human security in every area our top priority. This is the way to defeat war and violence at the most fundamental level.

Promoting a Global Awareness for a New Century of the Spirit

Ikeda: The Soviet cosmonaut Alexandr A. Serebrov (1944–2013) shared an interesting insight with me suggestive for the transformation of the human consciousness that we need. He took part in four space missions and performed ten space walks.

He said that each time he returned from a space journey, as soon as the lock of the craft opened, he was most strongly impressed with the aroma of the planet, the fresh smell of Earth. And when ships arrived at the space station, one could smell the aroma of the Earth and the wind on the door lock.

The Earth is the mother of all living things. We need to promote education to foster citizens of the Earth who respect and care for the planet that is our common home.

Esquivel: Definitely!

Terrorism, conflicts, and nuclear armaments threaten our common home, this small planet called Earth.

We have no other home. We must care for and respect our Mother Earth—its seas, its forests and plants, and the biological diversity of all living beings that are part of our planetary life.

Ikeda: Our movement's founder, Tsunesaburo Makiguchi, believed that one's local environment is very important.

He opposed both narrow-minded nationalism and superficial cosmopolitanism and insisted that people should start by learning about the place where they actually lived their lives, their local environment. His educational philosophy was to then steadily expand from that knowledge of the local to a wider and wider scale, fostering global citizens.

For example, he suggested that parents might start by looking at the cotton garments their children were wearing, and consider that they were only made possible by the labors of cotton growers perspiring under the hot Indian sun. His teaching was to encourage people to make concrete observations about their own lives, and then explore how their immediate environment linked them to the world as a whole.

Mr. Makiguchi wrote: "Our lives rely on the world, our home is the world, and the world is our sphere of activity."[12]

For him, education must make each person aware of belonging to their immediate local communities, their nation, and the world. It was an education that sought to make local and global awareness bulwarks preventing us from being swept away by the evils of nationalism at a time when the sole emphasis in Japan was on national awareness.

Such a view is essential, I believe, to the creation of a "society of global neighbors," the global society that is sought today.

In the light of the history of conflict among nations and with a view to a brighter future, Mr. Makiguchi also advocated a shift from military, political, and economic competition to "humanitarian competition."

I believe that the ideas of Makiguchi, who died in prison in his struggle against Japanese militarist authorities, offer important lessons for humanity's future course.

Esquivel: In the course of evolution, human beings have traveled different paths in prayer and meditation, but in the end the power of the spirit takes humanity to the right point.

The French philosopher Pierre Teilhard de Chardin (1881–1955) called this the Omega point, where all spiritual paths converge.

The infinite grace of God guides each individual there.

In addition to seeking the answers to the mysteries and secrets of the universe, we must humbly delve into our inner realm. Unless we open ourselves not only to the external but also the inner world, our ability to see life will be partial and distorted.

Ikeda: Pierre Teilhard de Chardin foresaw the arrival of a century of the mind and the spirit. Thinkers around the world have pursued the essence of the cosmos and of humanity in their own ways.

I am reminded of the reflections of the philosopher Immanuel Kant (1724–1804), whose works Mr. Makiguchi was reading right up until his death in prison: "Two things fill the mind with ever new and increasing wonder and awe, the oftener and the more steadily we reflect on them: the starry heavens above me and the moral law within me."[13]

In Buddhism, Shakyamuni attained insight into the depths of his own, vast, inner universe and, integrating it with the great external universe, perceived the life force that is the foundation of both the inner and outer universes.

Later Buddhists continued in the lineage of Shakyamuni's enlightenment. One of them was Vasubandhu, who lived in India around the fourth century. While personally experiencing Shakyamuni's inner insight, he also systemized the realm of the deep layers of the inner universe in what is called the teaching of the eight consciousnesses.

According to this teaching, the mind is made up of eight kinds of consciousness. In order from outermost to innermost layer, Vasubandhu began with the five consciousnesses (the five senses of sight, hearing, smell, taste, and touch). The sixth consciousness, called mind-consciousness, integrates the five sense consciousnesses, creates a mental image of the external world, and makes judgments about it. These six consciousnesses refer to the ordinary conscious functions of the self.

From the seventh or *mano*-consciousness, we enter a deeper level of self-awareness. It can be regarded as corresponding to the Western notion of the self. It represents the inner or spiritual realm and is the source of an individual's concept of identity.

Finally, the eighth consciousness, the *alaya*-consciousness, is the "treasury" in which the individual's karma is stored. It forms the underlying current of life that flows in relationships with other beings. In the first seven consciousnesses, both bad and good mental states function in tandem. Bad mental states include lust for power, hatred, greed, and egoism, and examples of good mental states are compassion, altruism, self-control, empathy, and nonviolence.

Buddhism further perceives that the good and bad latent energies that occasionally manifest themselves as good and bad mental states can be found as good and bad karma in the realm of the *alaya*-consciousness.

According to Mahayana teachings, the altruistic, empathetic way of the bodhisattva reinforces the good karma in the *alaya*-consciousness and makes possible the perception of the fundamental life force of the universe.

This realm probably corresponds to what you call spirituality.

Esquivel: Yes. Buddhism arrives at truly profound insights into the inner world.

Ikeda: Zhiyi, known as the Great Teacher Tiantai, in China and Nichiren in Japan refer to a ninth consciousness, the fundamental pure consciousness or *amala*-consciousness. This fundamental life force of the universe embraces the *alaya*-consciousness that is the underlying current of the individual life.

Buddhism identifies this with the Buddha nature or essential nature of phenomena, and because this great life is inherent in all people, all are worthy of respect. The Buddha nature—the ninth consciousness—can be found in the depths of the inner universe of each human life and, while one with the external universe, is the fundamental pure consciousness shining with compassion and wisdom.

This fundamental life underlying the eight consciousnesses is Nam-myoho-renge-kyo, referred to by Nichiren as "the palace of the ninth consciousness, the unchanging reality that reigns over all life's functions."[14]

Buddhism teaches us how to live so as to understand the basic power of life and the fundamental wisdom of the universe and in this way to make our lives radiant. In terms of an individual's life, this is the principle of human revolution, and in terms of society, the path to building peace.

Peace Is Born from the Capacity to See What Cannot Be Seen

Esquivel: I am reminded of an African proverb: "If you don't know where you're going, go back to find out where you come from." When along our journey through life we lose sight of our destination, returning to our starting point helps us see where we are going.

Of course we cannot know what our destination will be or what we will encounter along the way, but if our spirits are open to the four winds of liberty, love, peace, and justice, we can reaffirm our common spirituality.

Ikeda: No matter what happens, we must keep in mind the starting point. President Makiguchi always said that when you reach an impasse, you must return to your starting point. The starting point to which the human race must return is a genuinely human spirituality.

Esquivel: We should know how to see what exists but is invisible to our eyes, to discover the spirit inhabiting each of us.

Some time ago, I told a group of young people that I had recently found a piece of writing by a Nicaraguan woman who had been taken prisoner during the dictatorship of General Anastasio Somoza (1925–80). It brought to my mind the following chronicle about a Uruguayan political prisoner:

> The Uruguayan political prisoners may not talk without permission or whistle, smile, sing, walk fast, or greet other prisoners; nor may they make or receive drawings of pregnant women, couples, butterflies, stars, or birds.
>
> One Sunday, Didako Perez, school teacher, tortured and jailed "for having ideological ideas," is visited by his daughter Milay, age five. She brings him a drawing of birds. The guards destroy it at the entrance of the jail.
>
> On the following Sunday, Milay brings him a drawing of trees. Trees are not forbidden, and the drawing gets through. Didako praises her work and asks about the colored circles scattered in the treetops, many small circles half-hidden among the branches: "Are they oranges? What fruit is it?" The child puts her finger to her mouth "Shh."
>
> And she whispers in his ear: "Silly, don't you see they're eyes? They're the eyes of the birds that I've smuggled in for you."[15]

Can we see what is hidden in our hearts and minds?

Each of us must return to our interior realm and let the wind and silence in—open our hearts and allow them free entry, so as to return to our common home.

We follow different roads in search of the "land of no evil," the promised land where we can build our common home. If we do not know where our house is, it is because we are lost.

How do we find it? We must seek a road to the common home of the human family, and that road is the road of spirituality and the road of peace.

There is no home without spirituality. It is within ourselves, in our interior realm that we must awaken to compassion.

Without compassion, we will not find the road to our common home.

Ikeda: How true that is. And what a beautiful, inspiring story.

We must return to our true roots—the "common home" you speak of, the starting point for all human beings, transcending ethnicity and nationality. To accomplish that, we must change our way of life at the most fundamental level, to one of harmonious cooperation aiming for the happiness of both ourselves and other people.

You talk of searching for the "land of no evil" to build our common home. Where is that place?

In 1993, the year after the Los Angeles race riots, I visited the United States, where I dedicated to my friends there a long poem entitled "The sun of jiyu over a new land":

*As each group seeks their separate
roots and origins,
society fractures along a thousand fissure lines.
When neighbors distance themselves
from neighbors,
continue your uncompromising quest
for your truer roots
in the deepest regions of your lives.
Seek out the primordial "roots" of humankind.
Then you will without fail discover
the stately expanse of jiyu
unfolding in the depths of your life.*

*Here is the home, the dwelling place
to which humankind traces
its original existence—
beyond all borders,*

beyond all differences of gender and race.
Here is a world offering true proof
of our humanity.

If one reaches back to these fundamental roots,
all become friends and comrades.
To realize this is to "emerge from the earth."[16]

The Lotus Sutra, the core of Mahayana Buddhism, teaches that everyone is a part of the fundamental life force permeating all things and phenomena in the universe, endowed with inherent dignity. This essential nature of human beings is represented in the Lotus Sutra as great bodhisattvas who emerge from the earth (*jiyu*) to save all beings, the Bodhisattvas of the Earth.

The Bodhisattvas of the Earth possess four functions, manifesting the forces of the universe as symbolized by the four traditional elements of fire, wind, water, and earth.

First, like fire that blazes heavenward, illuminating everything around, they lead forward along the right path, igniting courage in people's hearts and dispelling darkness with the light of wisdom.

Second, like wind that blows boundlessly, they drive all obstacles from their paths, moving freely and unrestrictedly with powerful life force.

Third, like cool, clear, flowing water, they possess an undefiled and pure life, flowing into and cleansing our society rife with anger, greed, and other earthly desires.

Fourth, like the earth that nurtures all growing things, they protect all people with impartiality and manifest compassion to all equally.

These fundamental forces of life are inherent in all people. The human revolution we aim for is the process of fully tapping and manifesting those powers within both ourselves and other people.

The four powers of the Bodhisattvas of the Earth are also essential qualities in good leaders.

Driving the Culture of Violence from Our Hearts

Esquivel: That is a truly beautiful poem, guiding us toward a knowledge of our primordial identity. You know the common home of humanity, the abode to which we belong beyond our differences, which must be appreciated and well received in the heart and mind.

Many people ask whether peace is possible in a world rocked by war. People wonder whether peace is a Utopia, a dream humanity can never realize.

Today war seems to be the only way, closing off all other options; in the face of such times, we ask everyone, including ourselves, this question.

We must re-create spirit and conscience by freeing ourselves, banishing from within the violence that has dominated and enslaved us, that culture of violence by which we have been subjugated. Only then can we build a culture of peace.

Ikeda: I agree completely. That is the human revolution we speak of. The revitalization and transformation of the spirit of a single individual is the turning point from violence to peace.

At the same time, expanding a movement of the people based on humanism is crucial in shifting society from the path of violence to the path of peace. Such a movement is the force for changing society. It is a source of mutual inspiration and leads to spiritual transformation.

Through Nichiren Buddhism, Mr. Makiguchi urged the need to focus on people, to give them hope, and to join with them in common cause. He called for the establishment of a true humanism grounded in the worth and dignity of life and creating a movement based on nonviolence and compassion.

Tolstoy expressed the same idea in *War and Peace*: "My idea is just that if vicious people unite together into a power, then honest folk must do the same. That's simple enough, isn't it?"[17]

I firmly believe that a powerful movement of the people committed to transforming hatred into compassion and violence into nonviolence can build a culture of peace, and in that way the human race will finally break free from the chains of the cycle of war and violence.

Esquivel: You speak of Mr. Makiguchi, who was eager to establish an authentic humanism in which respect for human dignity was ingrained. As he indicated with great accuracy, we must turn our attention to humanity, provide people with hope, and seek to unite them.

How can we achieve these aims? The challenge is great. But often the solutions are simple. If we only could practice what Mr. Makiguchi said, values and attitudes toward life would change radically.

Youth's Mission to Build Peace

Esquivel: As you know well, we live in a unipolar world rife with conflicts: wars, hunger, and social, cultural, political, and economic inequalities. But the new generations must understand and take part in the struggle to build a different society.

What will that different society be? A society in which peace is the pillar of social, political, economic, and spiritual life, and in which horrors like Hiroshima and Nagasaki, concentration camps, wars, and the destruction of life never occur again.

The younger generations of today were not alive in that era when the irrationality of the power of destruction and death were unleashed by governments who thought the world was theirs. We must remember that the tragic events of the past are not gone forever, and though now concealed and latent, they have not disappeared.

Young people today have the mission of creating spaces for harmonious coexistence and mutual respect among individuals and peoples. To do that, they must cultivate spiritual fortitude.

Ikeda: It is true that the past has not disappeared. That is precisely why people who fought the abominable violence of the twentieth century, the century of war, must transmit the spirit of peace to the youth who will create the twenty-first century.

A month after September 11, 2001, Dr. Rotblat, who was ninety-two at the time, flew from London to Soka University of America in Aliso Viejo, California. He came to our campus, dedicated to cultivating people devoted to the peace of the world, eager to address students of the university's first entering class, burning with a sense of mission.

Identifying the Holocaust and the nuclear bombings of Hiroshima and Nagasaki as emblematic of the deleterious heritage of the twentieth century, Dr. Rotblat declared that they were made possible by a detestable underlying attitude of disregard and contempt for life and asserted that the same was true of the recent terrorist attacks. He went on to express his belief in the fundamental importance of a philosophy of the sanctity of life, and that we must change our orientation from the pursuit of ethnic and national interests to the pursuit of the interests of humanity as a whole.

He added that he believed in the goodness of humanity and its capability for civilized evolution.

You also visited Soka University in Japan and delivered a speech to students there (1994). That occasion was a tremendous inspiration to our students, who still speak about it today as a very rewarding event.

Esquivel: Thank you very much. It was an honor to visit Soka University.

The Soka Gakkai, the parent organization of Soka University, has endured attacks and persecutions for the sake of defending peace and justice since it was founded by President Makiguchi and continuing throughout the terms of the first three presidents. We have also struggled for peace and justice. I believe that this is an important point we share in common.

It is said that youth are the future, but I think that youth are also the present, the now, and the today. What youth are doing at present determines the future. The future is the direct consequence of the present. We will harvest the fruits tomorrow of the seeds we have the courage to sow today.

For this reason, young people must learn history and cultivate a critical awareness. Youth can open the doors of tomorrow. They can do it either with weapons in their hands or with arms outstretched in hope and brotherhood. Peace must be built by each young person and cultivated in the comradeship of peoples.

Human dignity can only be affirmed by the underlying awareness that we are all human beings. This is fostered by taking the initiative to act for the sake of our fellow human beings and society.

Human rights are nothing special or separate from daily life; on the contrary, we must always bear in mind that they are just our behavior as human beings. I hope that young people can cultivate and develop that awareness and that sense of responsibility.

A Life in Which Deeds Match Words Is an Example for the World

Esquivel: In Latin America, our SERPAJ, together with certain Swedish organizations, is conducting a disarmament campaign. Placing special emphasis on young people, its efforts are directed toward schools and the development of awareness of the consequences of arms and the necessity of disarmament. We teach that violence is not an acceptable way of life.

We must resolve our conflicts through dialogue, not violence. We encourage practicing this principle in daily life as individuals, in families, communities, countries, and throughout the world.

Utopias always require effort and great hope. This is something that Mr. Toda also emphasized.

Ikeda: Thank you for your understanding of my mentor.

One of Mr. Toda's timeless messages to us is his insistence that a new era is created by the passion and power of youth.

You and all the other world thinkers with whom I have shared dialogues agree that the future of humanity rests on the shoulders of youth.

We are committed to focusing with even greater intensity on young people and building a movement of the people dedicated to taking action to resolve our global problems.

Esquivel: The SGI contributes to the formation of youth and its organizations in each country, and its members are paradigms of life, peace, and respect.

You, President Ikeda, are a person whose words and deeds are consistent. You put your words into action and impart spiritual strength to those around you. I hope that you will continue your work for the good of humanity for many years to come.

On one occasion, I told young people of SGI-Argentina how important it was to put into practice the teachings of Mr. Ikeda:

Everything President Ikeda conveys to you derives from his commitment as a builder of peace and contains great wisdom. I urge you to put into practice in your various arenas of action the values and principles of spirituality and wisdom that President Ikeda has imparted to you. They will enable you to change your reality and society. Action is fundamental.

Ikeda: You are too kind. And I am deeply grateful for your warm encouragement of young people. The courage that your words of wisdom and faith as a peace activist have imparted to young people is beyond measure.

I have also learned much from this dialogue with you.

A Buddhist scripture teaches, "If you want to understand the causes that existed in the past, look at the results as they are manifested in the present. And if you want to understand what results will be manifested in the future, look at the causes that exist in the present."[18]

As we tread the unwavering path of peace and justice together with you and our young people, let us create causes of future hope and triumph.

For the sake of humanity, I wholeheartedly pray for your long life and increasingly good health.

Notes

1. The Struggle for Human Rights—A Story of Glorious Triumph

1. See "The Nobel Peace Prize 1980—Presentation Speech," www. nobelprize.org/nobel_prizes/peace/laureates/1980/presentation-speech.html (accessed April 25, 2017).
2. Translated from Japanese. Dr. Esquivel's interview appears in the November 23, 1996, *Seikyo Shimbun,* the Soka Gakkai's daily newspaper.
3. Translated from Spanish. Patricio Aylwin and Daisaku Ikeda, *Alborada del Pacífico* (Dawn of the Pacific), ed. Fundación Konrad Adenauer (Santiago, Chile: Centro de Acción Internacional, Centro de Estudios, Universidad Miguel de Cervantes, 2002), p. 18.
4. Ibid., p. 19.
5. Ibid.
6. Mahatma Gandhi, *The Collected Works of Mahatma Gandhi,* vol. 18 (Ahmedabad: Publications Division, Ministry of Information and Broadcasting, Government of India, 1990), p. 133.
7. Plato, *The Republic,* ed. G. R. F. Ferrari, trans. Tom Griffith (Cambridge: Cambridge University Press, 2003), p. 201.
8. Translated from Japanese. Tsunesaburo Makiguchi, *Makiguchi Tsunesaburo zenshu* (Complete Works of Tsunesaburo Makiguchi), vol. 10 (Tokyo: Daisanbunmei-sha, 1987), p. 30.

9. Translated from Japanese. "Sekai no shikisha to kataru—Esukiberu hakase" (Recollections of My Meetings with Leading World Figures—Dr. Esquivel), January 19, 1997, *Seikyo Shimbun.*

10. Victor Hugo, *Les Misérables,* trans. Lee Fahnestock and Norman MacAfee (New York: New American Library, 1987), p. 214.

11. Osaka Incident: The occasion when Mr. Ikeda, then Soka Gakkai youth division chief of staff, was arrested and wrongfully charged with election law violations in a House of Councilors by-election in Osaka in 1957. At the end of the court case, which dragged on for almost five years, he was fully exonerated of all charges.

12. Nichiren, *The Writings of Nichiren Daishonin,* vol. 1 (Tokyo: Soka Gakkai, 1999), p. 579.

13. Translated from Japanese. Kunio Yanagita, *Teihon Yanagita Kunio shu* (The Complete Works of Kunio Yanagita), vol. 3 (Tokyo: Chikuma Shobo, 1978), p. 463.

14. Makiguchi, *Makiguchi Tsunesaburo zenshu*, vol. 10, pp. 201–2.

15. Jawaharlal Nehru, *The Discovery of India* (New Delhi: Jawaharlal Nehru Memorial Fund, 1995), p. 442.

16. This refers to a counter-summit held by the world's poorest nations, which held that the fifteenth annual conference of industrialized countries (1989 G7 summit) neglected Third World issues. This alternative gathering was organized by the International League for the Rights and Liberation of Peoples, a pressure group led by Dr. Esquivel.

17. Plato, *The Dialogues of Plato,* vol. 2, trans. B. Jowett (Oxford: The Clarendon Press, 1892), p. 419.

18. Nichiren, *The Writings of Nichiren Daishonin,* vol. 1, p. 767.

19. Cf. Hideo Hirose, "Nichiren shonin 'tatsunokuchi' honan no toki no tenpen ni tsuite" (The Honorable Nichiren and Extraordinary Phenomena in the Heavens during the Tatsunokuchi Persecution) in *Tenmon to kisho* (Astronomy and Weather) (Tokyo: Chijin Shokan Co., Ltd., 1956), p. 14.

20. Nichiren, *The Writings of Nichiren Daishonin,* vol. 1, p. 767.

21. Albert Camus, *The Myth of Sisyphus* (New York: Vintage Books, 1991), p. 66.

22. *The Group of Discourses (Sutta-Nipāta),* trans. K. R. Norman (Oxford: The Pali Text Society Oxford, 2001), p. 56.

23. Nichiren, *The Writings of Nichiren Daishonin,* vol. 1, p. 4.

2. A World United by the Power of the People

1. Translated from Spanish. Eduardo Mallea, *Historia de una Pasión Argentina* (The History of an Argentine Passion) (Buenos Aires: Editorial Sudamericana, 1961), p. 160.

2. Nichiren, *The Writings of Nichiren Daishonin,* vol. 2 (Tokyo: Soka Gakkai, 2006), p. 809.

3. Ibid., p. 318.

4. José Hernández, *The Gaucho Martín Fierro,* trans. C. E. Ward (New York: State University of New York Press, 1967), p. 491.

5. Lao Tzu, *The Sayings of Lao Tzu,* trans. Lionel Giles (London: John Murray, 1950), p. 51.

6. Johann Wolfgang von Goethe, *Faust,* trans. Walter Arndt (New York: W. W. Norton & Company, Inc., 1976), p. 30.

7. Ibid., p. 294.

8. Arnold J. Toynbee, *Acquaintances* (London: Oxford University Press, 1967), p. 294.

9. Translated from Japanese. Dr. Esquivel's remarks appear in the November 10, 1988, *Yomiuri Shimbun.*

10. Translated from Japanese. Mr. Bobbio's remarks appear in the September 1, 1997, *Asahi Shimbun.*

11. *The Word of the Doctrine (Dhammapada),* trans. K. R. Norman (Oxford: The Pali Text Society, 2000), p. 24.

12. Translated from Sanskrit. "Udānavarga," see www.ancient-buddhist-texts.net/Buddhist-Texts/S1-Udanavarga/S1-Udanavarga.pdf (accessed November 29, 2016).

13. See Food and Agricultural Organization (FAO), "FAO Warns World Cannot Afford Hunger" (September 14, 2005), www.fao.org/

newsroom/en/news/2005/107538/index.html (accessed December 7, 2017).

14. Translated from Japanese. Patricio Aylwin Azócar and Daisaku Ikeda, "Taiheiyo no kyokujitsu" (Dawn of the Pacific) in *Ikeda Daisaku zenshu* (Collected Writings of Daisaku Ikeda), vol. 108 (Tokyo: Seikyo Shimbun-sha, 2004), p. 163.

15. See Jawaharlal Nehru, *Selected Works of Jawaharlal Nehru,* Second Series, vol. 3 (New Delhi: Jawaharlal Nehru Memorial Fund, 1985), p. 136.

16. *The Lotus Sutra and Its Opening and Closing Sutras,* trans. Burton Watson (Tokyo: Soka Gakkai, 2009), p. 309.

17. Arnold J. Toynbee, *East to West: A Journey Round the World* (London: Oxford University Press, 1958), p. 22.

18. See Ministry of Foreign Affairs of Japan, "Argentine Republic," 2009. www.mofa.go.jp/mofaj/area/argentine/data.html (accessed September 21, 2009).

19. Translated from Japanese. Natalio Gorin, *Piasora: Jishin o kataru* (Astor Piazzolla: A Memoir) (Tokyo: Kawade Shobo Shinsha, 2006), p. 47.

20. Translated from Japanese. Mr. Pugliese's remarks appear in the February 12, 1995, *Seikyo Shimbun.*

21. Translated from Japanese. Toson Shimazaki, *Toson bunmei ronshu* (Toson's Essays on Civilization), ed. Shinsuke Togawa (Tokyo: Iwanami Shoten, 1988), p. 143.

22. An oasis town located in the Kansu Province, China, where religious, cultural, and artistic treasures are preserved in the form of painting and sculpture in its Mogao Caves (also known as the Cave of the Thousand Buddhas).

23. Nichiren, *The Writings of Nichiren Daishonin,* vol. 2, p. 1060.

3. Transmitting the Legacy of Nonviolence

1. Albert Einstein, *The Quotable Einstein,* ed. Alice Calaprice (New Jersey: Princeton University Press, 1996), p. 66.

2. Translated from Japanese. Jawaharlal Nehru, *Jiyu to heiwa eno michi* (The Path to Freedom and Peace), trans. Shinichi Inoue (Tokyo: Shakai shiso kenkyu kai, 1952), p. 149.

3. M. K. Gandhi, *An Autobiography: The Story of My Experiments with Truth,* trans. Mahadev Desai (London: Penguin Books, 1982), p. 274.

4. R. K. Prabhu, *This Was Bapu* (Ahmedabad: Navajivan Trust, 1954), p. 12.

5. Raghavan N. Iyer, *The Moral and Political Thought of Mahatma Gandhi* (Oxford: Oxford University Press, 1973), p. 226.

6. Translated from German. Friedrich Hölderlin, "Hyperion" in *Sämtliche Werke* (Collected Works), vol. 3, ed. Friedrich Beissner (Stuttgart: W. Kohlhammer Verlag, 1957), p. 14.

7. Dante Alighieri, *The Divine Comedy,* vol. 1, trans. Mark Musa (New York: Penguin Books, 1984), p. 83.

8. N. Radhakrishnan and Daisaku Ikeda, *Walking with the Mahatma: Gandhi for Modern Times* (New Delhi: Eternal Ganges Press, 2015), pp. 160–1.

9. Mahatma Gandhi, *All Men Are Brothers: Autobiographical Reflections,* ed. Krishna Kripalani (New York: The Continuum Publishing Company, 2000), p. 136.

10. Cf. Tiantai, *Great Concentration and Insight.* This means that the bodhisattva seeks enlightenment while remaining immersed in the real world, teaching the Buddhist Law to others.

11. Translated from Japanese. *Taisho shinshu daizokyo* (Taisho Tripitaka) (Tokyo: Taisho Shinshu Daizokyo Publishing Society, 1924–34), vol. 25, p. 86.

12. Ibid.

13. *Chuang Tzu: Basic Writings,* trans. Burton Watson (New York: Columbia University Press, 1996), p. 140.

14. Krishna Kripalani, *Gandhi: A Life* (Delhi: National Book Trust, 1968), p. 181.

15. World of desire: The first division of the threefold world—the world of unenlightened beings who transmigrate within the six paths (from

hell through the realm of heavenly beings). The threefold world consists of, in ascending order, the world of desire, the world of form, and the world of formlessness. It is called the world of desire because its inhabitants are ruled by various desires. The world of desire comprises the four evil paths of existence (the realms of hell, hungry spirits, animals, and *asuras*), the four continents (the realm of human beings) surrounding Mount Sumeru, and the six heavens (the realm of heavenly beings) of the world of desire.

16. Martin Luther King, Jr., *Where Do We Go from Here: Chaos or Community?* (New York: Harper & Row, 1967), p. 128.
17. Gandhi, *All Men Are Brothers,* p. viii.
18. Krishna Kripalani, *Gandhi: A Life,* p. 77.

4. The Crucial Role of Women in the Century of Life

1. Translated from Japanese. Dr. Radhakrishnan's speech appears in the April 12, 2007, *Seikyo Shimbun.*
2. Gandhi, *All Men Are Brothers*, p. 148.
3. Translated from Japanese. "Meiyo kaicho no Indo no jinken toso o meguru katarai" (President Ikeda's Conversations with Youth—The Struggle for Human Rights in India), June 15, 1993, *Seikyo Shimbun.*
4. Translated from Japanese. Mrs. Parks' speech at Soka University Los Angeles campus, Calabasas, on December 5, 1992, appears in the January 6, 1993, *Seikyo Shimbun.*
5. Rosa Parks and Gregory J. Reed, *Dear Mrs. Parks: A Dialogue with Today's Youth* (New York: Lee & Low Books, Inc., 1996), p. 97.
6. Translated from Japanese. Ms. Menchú's interview appears in the October 3, 1993, *Seikyo Shimbun.*
7. Nichiren, *The Writings of Nichiren Daishonin,* vol. 2, p. 844.
8. Ibid., p. 931.
9. This principle refers to the actions of bodhisattvas who, though qualified to receive the pure rewards of Buddhist practice, relinquish them and make a vow to be reborn in an impure world

in order to save living beings. They spread the Mystic Law, while undergoing the same sufferings as those born in the evil world due to karma. It derives from Miaole's interpretation of the passage in "The Teacher of the Law" chapter of the Lotus Sutra, which reads "Medicine King, you should understand that these people voluntarily relinquish the reward due them for their pure deeds and, in the time after I [the Buddha] have passed into extinction, because they pity living beings, they are born in this evil world so they may broadly expound this sutra."

10. *The World Reshaped—Volume 1: Fifty Years after the War in Europe,* ed. Richard Cobbold (London: Macmillan Press Ltd., 1996), p. 31.

11. M. K. Gandhi, *Women and Social Injustice* (Ahmedabad: Navajivan Publishing House, 1954), p. 18.

12. Translated from Japanese. Coudenhove-Kalergi, *Kudenhofu Karerugi zenshu* (Collected Works of Coudenhove-Kalergi), vol. 2, ed. Morinosuke Kajima and Eiichi Fukatsu (Kagoshima: Kajima Institute Publishing Co., Ltd., 1970), p. 398.

13. Rabindranath Tagore, *The English Writings of Rabindranath Tagore,* vol. 2, ed. Sisir Kumar Das (New Delhi: Sahitya Akademi, 1996), pp. 412, 416.

14. The CEDAW, adopted in 1979 by the UN General Assembly.

15. Eve Curie, *Madame Curie,* ed. P. E. Charvet (Cambridge, UK: Cambridge University Press, 1942), p. 122.

16. Susan Quinn, *Marie Curie: A Life* (Cambridge, Massachusetts: Perseus Books, 1996), p. 418.

17. Shrimala: A daughter of King Prasenajit of Kosala and his consort Mallika, in the time of Shakyamuni, Shrimala married Mitrayashas (also known as Yashomitra), the king of Ayodhya. She is the protagonist of the Shrimala Sutra, which depicts her conversion to Buddhism by her parents, her encounter with Shakyamuni, and her vows to the Buddha to propagate the one vehicle teaching.

18. *The Sutra of Queen Srīmālā of the Lion's Roar,* trans. Diana Y. Paul (Berkeley, California: Numata Center for Buddhist Translation and Research, 2004), p. 15.

19. *The Lion's Roar of Queen Srimala,* trans. Alex and Hideko Wayman (New Delhi: Motilal Banarsidass Publishers Private Limited, 2007), p. 64.
20. Nichiren, *The Writings of Nichiren Daishonin,* vol. 1, p. 24.
21. *The Lotus Sutra and Its Opening and Closing Sutras,* p. 227.
22. Nichiren, *The Writings of Nichiren Daishonin,* vol. 1, p. 464.
23. Ibid., p. 385. "The Latter Day of the Law" refers to the age when the teachings of Shakyamuni lose the power to lead people to enlightenment. It was generally regarded to mean the period two thousand years after the Buddha's passing. In Japan, it was believed that this age began in the year 1052.
24. Translated from Japanese. *Nichiren Daishonin gosho zenshu* (The Complete Works of Nichiren Daishonin), ed. Nichiko Hori (Tokyo: Soka Gakkai, 1952), p. 813.
25. *The Group of Discourses (Sutta-Nipāta),* p. 18.
26. Translated from Japanese. Tsunesaburo Makiguchi, *Makiguchi Tsunesaburo zenshu* (Complete Works of Tsunesaburo Makiguchi), vol. 6 (Tokyo: Daisanbunmei-sha, 1983), p. 14.
27. Translated from Japanese. "Katei no tanoshimi" (The Joys of Family Life) in *Daikatei,* vol. 3 (1) (Tokyo: Dainippon Koto Jogakkai, 1907), pp. 2, 4.
28. See UNESCO Institute for Statistics, "International Literacy Day 2005," www.unescobkk.org/fileadmin/user_upload/efa/EFA_News/UIS_factsheet_05Literacy.pdf (accessed September 13, 2017).
29. Ralph Waldo Emerson, *Miscellanies* (Boston: Houghton, Mifflin and Company, 1884), pp. 283–4.
30. Translated from Japanese. Mariane Pearl, *Maiti haato* (A Mighty Heart), trans. Tato Takahama (Tokyo: Ushio Publishing Co., Ltd., 2005), p. 425.

5. Youth—The Key to Building a Culture of Peace

1. Translated from Japanese. Mr. Ikeda's remarks based on a well-known passage from Confucius appear in the January 5, 2008, *Seikyo Shimbun.*

2. Translated from Japanese, Richard von Weizsäcker, *Rekishi ni me o tozasuna: Vaitsuzekka Nihon koenroku* (Don't Shut Your Eyes to History: Collected Speeches of Weizsäcker in Japan), trans. Kiyohiko Nagai (Tokyo: Iwanami Shoten, 1996), p. 143.

3. Albert Einstein, *Out of My Later Years* (New York: Philosophical Library, 1950), p. 185.

4. Ibid., p. 188.

5. Ibid., p. 190.

6. Daisaku Ikeda, "Humanizing Religion, Creating Peace," 2008 Peace Proposal: www.daisakuikeda.org/assets/files/pp2008.pdf (accessed December 15, 2017).

7. Josei Toda, "Declaration Calling for the Abolition of Nuclear Weapons," www.joseitoda.org/vision/declaration/read.html (accessed December 15, 2017).

8. Translated from Japanese. Dr. Rotblat's speech appears in the February 11, 2000, *Seikyo Shimbun*.

9. Translated from Japanese. Mr. ElBaradei's remarks appear in the December 1, 2006, *Seikyo Shimbun*.

10. Ibid.

11. Translated from Japanese. Dr. Swaminathan's remarks appear in the July 14, 2004, *Seikyo Shimbun*.

12. Translated from Japanese. Tsunesaburo Makiguchi, *Makiguchi Tsunesaburo zenshu* (Complete Works of Tsunesaburo Makiguchi), vol. 1 (Tokyo: Daisanbunmei-sha, 1983), p. 26.

13. Immanuel Kant, *Critique of Practical Reason,* trans. Lewis White Beck (New York: MacMillan Publishing Company, 1993), p. 169.

14. Nichiren, *The Writings of Nichiren Daishonin,* vol. 1, p. 832.

15. Thomas L. Jackson, *Moments of Clarity* (Indiana: Xlibris Corporation, 2001), pp. 77–8.

16. Daisaku Ikeda, *Journey of Life: Selected Poems of Daisaku Ikeda* (London: I.B. Tauris, 2014), p. 241.

17. Leo Tolstoy, *War and Peace,* trans. Rosemary Edmonds (New York: Penguin Books, 1987), p. 1397.

18. Nichiren, *The Writings of Nichiren Daishonin,* vol. 1, p. 279.

Index

Milton Keynes UK
Ingram Content Group UK Ltd.
UKHW021844171124
451196UK00004B/134